MW01532850

Design, Layout, and Assistant Editing by Tara Thorenson

# Fixing Broken

## a **TRUE STORY** by

*Barbara Medina*

# TABLE OF CONTENTS

# TABLE OF CONTENTS

*My story is dedicated to all of my fellow adoptees who struggle to know themselves...*
*You are not alone.*

# Introduction

*It's March of 2018 and by now I've been working as a full time Hairstylist for over 30 years, so blessed with a faithful clientele of wonderful customers. Also, I'm the proud homeowner of a nice little property where I've devised the perfect work-from-home situation. I've been told by those who visit that my curb appeal with its quaint, doted on gardens feels like a hug when approaching. Here, I've created my sanctuary with the things that inspire me, including my two adored Pugs.*

*My inner circle of close friends has been carefully cultivated over the years and to those especially close to me, I'm considered one of the family. My debt is low and my bills are paid on time. I had my act together, or at least that's how it looked to everyone else. Then quite suddenly on a late winter evening, my world turned upside. I have always had questions about my beginnings with few answers so, I eagerly embrace this new opportunity to finally find out where I come from...and why.*

*Both of my adoptive parents are gone now so I don't hold back. Instead, I dive headfirst into this new discovery with unguarded enthusiasm, eager to learn what has forever been hidden. But, as these events flowed into my life, I soon realized how lost I truly was.*

*Finding birth-family is one of those situations that for some reason, people seem to find it fascinating. As I continued to uncover new information, the theme I heard over and over again was, You need to write about this! But, it seemed strange to me to write about it, let alone share it for others just so they could be fascinated. Besides, what is really so fascinating?*

*As expected, there were some really incredible highs with all of this discovery but what I had not quite anticipated was, the lows that came were beyond bearable. I finally began writing because I needed it to be my therapy. Traditional therapy wasn't working and I knew I had to do something to lift the heaviness in my heart.*

*In order for it to make sense that these new discoveries were in deed fascinating, I had to shed light on why.*

*First, there was this beginning...a shaky one that had its own heartbreak. Adoption into a home with lots of potential but, instead there were too many roadblocks that brought a lifetime of uncertainty and pain pushed down where others hopefully couldn't see. I needed to write about that too because it's just as much of the story. Yes, there was this...but, because first, there was that.*

*To prepare myself to go there, to those past memories of so long ago, I'd sit in silence picturing the earliest moments I could recall. Our home, and all that I saw and felt. I was a bit surprised at how all of it had been kept stored — dying to be remembered. Songs kept popping up. The ones I heard as a child riding my bike through our neighborhood. The songs from the secret album sessions with my brother. Time spent singing along with childhood friends. Music that carried me from event to event. I found and downloaded these songs making a several hours long playlist. As I would prepare myself to write, the music helped to bring those memories forward to push me along the way. Most of it poured out in a hurry and as it did, I could breathe easier. Writing my story was what I needed to do — to see what I so badly needed to see but, couldn't...until it was written.*

*Please note, some names have been changed to protect the identity of those who wished to remain unnamed.*

# His Name Was Medina

Monday has been my day off for over thirty years. Over time, I have come to prefer my Sunday/Monday end of week over the typical Saturday/Sunday weekend with others rushing into Monday with weekend withdrawal. Instead, I enjoy the quiet morning with my coffee, gazing out the window at my bird feeders. I can ponder though my weeks schedule and later run errands with empty stores and near empty streets. Mondays have a feeling for me unlike the rest of the week that brings a calm and a slowness I have come to appreciate.

But, on this particular Monday, March 19, 2018, I couldn't begin to fathom how different this day would end from how it had started.

That day's temps actually reached into the low 40's causing the mounds of Minnesota snow to melt fast. Around here, we practically break out the shorts and T-shirts on late winter days like these. That morning and afternoon I did some bookkeeping, then headed to the store to replenish my supply of hair color and later made certain my bird feeders were full and the walkways were free of slush — all with the company of my two pugs, Mustang and Valentine, following closely.

Now its evening and I'm laid out on the couch watching The Voice, scrolling through my phone mindlessly. A new email with an unfamiliar address was waiting in my inbox. I clicked on it and as I read, I quickly shot up and grabbed my cheaters.

It's from a woman named DeDe Medina.

*"Hi I am Ruben Medina's stepdaughter. I found your email address online. Here's my phone number...please call me."*
So, Ruben was my birth-father's name?! Ruben. I've always loved the sandwich.

My mind was all over the place and I couldn't hit the numbers on my phone fast enough. Quickly, I turn off the TV. It's ringing…holding my breath, I hear and anxious sounding

*"Hello?"*
*"Hi, is this DeDe?"*

The woman's voice greeting me on the phone held such warmth and seemed to have the same amount of excitement to match mine.

The next couple of hours were like a waking dream. Recently, I had discovered that the non-identifying limited information I knew about my birth-father matched with a close DNA relative on my ancestry.com profile. A first cousin answered my message letting me know that my description of my birth-father sounded like her uncle who had passed away last year. His name was Medina. That is all I knew so far and now I'm on the phone with DeDe opening up a whole new world that I thought I'd never come to know about. She spoke fast…showing effort to stay calm.

*"Your Dad died just eleven months ago. My Mom was married to him for over fifty years. My sister Cindy and I are from a previous marriage but, he raised us so, he's Dad!"*

Ironic! He raised two unrelated daughters. All the while, someone else was raising his. Ruben had married their mother when she was pregnant with his daughter making a family of 5 in a short time. I'm not quite sure how long DeDe talked. Time was lost because I held on to every single word like it was gold. All of my senses were hyper focused on everything she said. She filled me in confirming that he was 100% Mexican, with both of his parents coming from Mexico. He was the oldest of 9 children growing up in Moline, Illinois where his family worked as migrant farmers and that he, with his brothers and sisters would be out in the fields working every summer. He spoke fluent Spanish, and after the training he received in the Air Force, worked most of his life as a machinist.

As DeDe talked, I absorbed her words internally, creating pictures to go with every description she gave. Seeing bright color and practically smelling smells and hearing sounds making it all come alive. This was the first glimpse of half of me. Where I came from. I could tell by DeDe's tone and the way she described him that she loved and cared about him very much. And that made me happy.

She asked when I was born and I told her... then there was a long stretch of silence on the phone. DeDe's excited voice became more serious.

*"Okay, I have to tell you something...and it's not good."*

I always assumed that my birth parents were young when they had me, which is why I was probably given up for adoption. I figured they would have both gone on to marry and have children, making it likely that I would have younger half siblings. Come to find out, Ruben was a married man, step-father to two and with one of his own when I came along. A product of infidelity. The limited non-identifying info our family received at my adoption outlined my birth-mother's age, origins, background and health history. Along with some loose details about how she met my birth-Dad and the little she knew about him. As far as I've always known, he never knew about me. As a child, I would fantasize about who my birth-parents were. In my fantasy world, they were beautiful! Dynamic... Movie star material. This information knocked the shine right off of my childhood dream.

*"You have a bunch of uncles and an aunt who live in Illinois and Iowa. I've lost track of how many cousins we have but, there's a lot!"*

After learning so much over those couple of hours, we ended with DeDe offering to send me pictures — the next day when she had time to sit down at her computer and go through them. We ended our phone call connected in a way I've never felt after one call with a stranger. Two hours latter with a head full of imagined faces and so much new information, I knew I needed to head off to bed to get some sleep.

How am I going to manage to wait till tomorrow to see my birth-Dad's face? I was so excited and worked up. I laid in bed imagining what he will look like. Do I look like him? I have to wait till tomorrow! Can I sleep at all tonight? My phone was in the kitchen charging, and after some time I heard a text come in. She didn't wait! She sent me a picture!! Bolting out of bed, I run through the dark to grab my phone. A text! YES!! I opened it…

And for the first time ever at the age of 54 years old, I laid eyes on my birth-father.

How do you recognize a face you've never seen before? And yet, I recognized that face. That's him…that's definitely him!

I stood there in the dark staring at his picture for a very long time. That night was a long sleepless one — not certain how long the tears fell before sleep finally came. The door to my secret past was now cracked open and I'm finally getting a peek.

Reuben

# Docile to a Fault

I was born in Los Angeles, CA the summer of 1964, actually during the time know as [1] The Baby Scoop Era. From 1945 to 1972 there were an estimated 4 million children given up for adoption in the US with 2 million during the 60's alone. I was among those many children who were placed into the state's hands to be adopted out. Vetting was done but, nothing like the vetting that goes on today with hopeful parents remaining on waiting lists for years with considerably fewer babies given up.

Before 1983, all of California's adoptions were completely non-identifying. Which meant, records were sealed with only a court order allowing them to be opened, keeping birth-families and adoptive families from knowing hardly anything about each other. This brought in women from other states where anonymity was not promised, wanting closed, secret adoptions where they could hope to avoid exposure. With such high numbers coming through the system, California had quite the task of finding suitable homes for all of those babies given up.

My adoptive parents, Norman and Marion Reddick were 35 and 39 respectively. Mom was actually older than Dad and almost aged out with 40 being the cut-off to adopt.

She grew up in St Louis, Missouri the oldest of five children with an alcoholic father. She was attractive and had a nice singing voice. After high school she did some professional modeling and also sang her way through nightclubs looking for fame and fortune. By her mid-20's she gave those dreams over and enlisted in the Marine Corps, looking for a new adventure.

---

1    The Baby Scoop Era Research Initiative; Research and Inquiry into adoption practices 1945-1972

Dad grew up in Columbia, South Carolina one of five boys including a set of twins with one not surviving past three years old. His family was poor but, full of southern kindness. Dad rarely spoke about his life, including his past but when he did, he used as few words as possible with no elaboration. Both Mom and Dad were born during the Great Depression, leaving its share of battle scars behind. After high school with no money for collage, Dad enlisted in the Marine Corps. A common path for those seeking an education provided by the GI bill.

Mom and Dad met there and were married two months later. After his four-year stint in the Marines, Dad attended college while Mom worked to support them. He latter graduated with a degree in Electrical Engineering. In those years, it was expected of married couples to have children. Mom and Dad spent over a decade trying to produce children on their own, to no avail.

13 years later with a two-year-old boy in tow, also adopted, they brought me home at three-months-old and we were a family complete.

Dad had acquired a good job and they had purchased a modest home in coveted Orange County where the American dream lived large. How could it get any better?

I don't doubt that my parents wanted children, yet their reasons were often a mystery growing up in their household. Evidence of their buyer's remorse showed up pretty early on. The air in our home was very heavy, both figuratively and literally. The smell of cigarettes permeated our entire house with both of them being pack-a-day smokers. Mom and Dad were strict with us in different ways. Dad was quiet…too quiet. A man of very few words who seemed to stay in a constant state of withdrawal. He suffered from agoraphobia, always avoiding large spaces and crowds. He tended to prefer not interacting with anyone and, always seemed happiest sitting alone in the dark in front of the TV. The drapes on the windows stayed drawn constantly. All of that California sunshine did not make its way into our home. I rarely knew where I stood with Dad. He didn't show an interest in knowing me...nor allowed me to really know him. Our home was strict and controlled. Not a drop of alcohol was ever allowed on the premise and this worked well for Mom, concerning her upbringing around alcoholism. Dad never touched the stuff and judged harshly those who did. Actually, anything he didn't approve of received his harsh criticism. If he found something disdainful, we were to find it so too.

Dad had a strong wall built up around him. That meant not coming to him with intention, words or needs. With others he carried a gentle spirit and humility, evident of his southern roots. But, his demeanor with me consistently showed intolerance. He actually tolerated very little that didn't fit into his understanding. Unlike Mom though, he was a very composed disciplinarian. Breaking the rules did not go unpunished. If caught, my brother and I would be sent outside to pull a switch from our rubber tree in the back yard. If I didn't pull an adequate one, he would pull one for me. I would get switched either on my butt or my legs. He would do it with control, not showing anger. I think my feelings were always hurt beyond my body.

My earliest memories of my Dad come at three years old. I remember him coming home from work in the evenings. He looked so handsome in his suit and smelled so good. We would gather in the living room after dinner to watch something like Gunsmoke, Daniel Boon or Star Trek on TV. If his mood provided, I'd crawl up onto his lap and sit with him. After some time, he would complain his legs were falling asleep and I would have to get down. I loved sitting on his lap, smelling his Old Spice mixed with tobacco. Feeling his cheek just starting to have a little stubble. Putting my arms around his neck, I wanted to sit with him longer...always a little bit longer. But, I did what I was told and would go sit on the sofa or the floor. Docile to a fault.

Mom found parenting very challenging. By the time I was 3 she had developed ulcers. High strung and reactive, she would talk about her nerves…it was always her nerves. Today, I'm sure the diagnosis would be "generalized anxiety." Apparently, caring for two young children was more than her nerves could handle and the ulcers were eating her alive.

Dad, always the problem solver, found a doctor who was doing an experimental in-office treatment promising to end the ulcers. Dad insisted Mom go to see him. When she hesitated, he accused her of not wanting to get well because she liked the attention. I will agree there was a spark of truth to Dad's claim but, she went along with his prompting — not to let him be right in lieu of having her reservations.

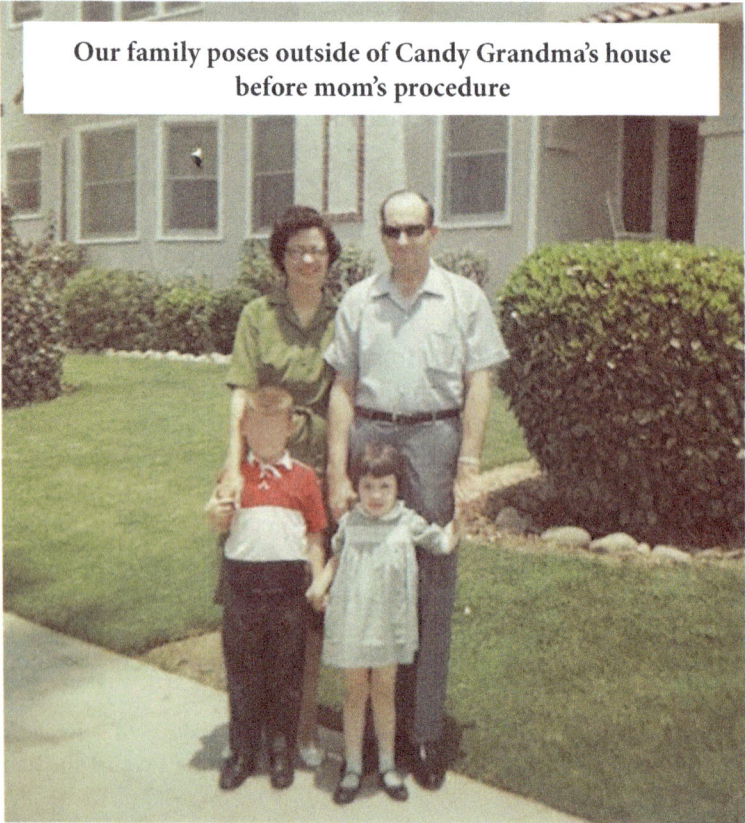

**Our family poses outside of Candy Grandma's house before mom's procedure**

# Mother's Little Helper

Mom was not afraid of the doctor's office mind you. She had managed to acquire the medicine she needed to calm her ever rustling nerves. I could always tell when Mom was on tranquilizers. Her speech would be slurred, her blinking slowed, her movements slower.

Dad never liked her taking them and they would fight about it. But, Mom held onto them very tightly and could always manage to score what she needed form her doctors. Sometimes, she would hit up our Pediatrician when she would bring us in to be seen. Those precious pills were "mother's little helper" indeed.

The day came when Dad took her in to have the ulcer ending procedure done. She was to swallow some sort of balloon that would go down into her stomach to be inflated with the hope of healing the ulcer. While swallowing the balloon, it had lodged and become stuck. She complained something didn't feel right but, the doctor insisted everything was fine and began inflating the balloon anyway — to which it then blew a hole in her esophagus and severely damaged her right lung. The doctor somehow found the procedure to be a success and even though she was still somewhat sedated, they sent her home.

My Grandma was watching me and my brother at her house. She lived in a fourplex on the second floor of an old beautiful building on a busy corner in South Pasadena. Huge palm trees lined both sides of her street and I remember how excited I would feel seeing them, knowing we were getting closer to her house. Grandma was a class act. Everything at her house was impeccable. She had beautiful, tasteful furniture and decor, taking much care for detail. A huge curved sofa sat in her living room and beautiful glass dishes were placed about filled with a variety of colorful candy. She was our "Candy" Grandma and in her presence, I always felt special.

On the way to pick us up after Mom's procedure, Mom told Dad she was having some difficulty breathing and wanted to lay down for a while before we all went home. When they walked through the door into the foyer, Mom immediately fainted and hit the floor. Dad was frantically slapping her cheek and calling her name, *"Marion!... Marion!!"*

Being only three years old, I was too young to really understand what I was seeing. I remember feeling quite detached. I didn't run to her like a little one might. Instead, I stood at the top of the stairs holding onto my brother's hand while Grandma and Dad tried to wake her. The ambulance came and rushed her off to the hospital where she spent the next few months. 32 operations and procedures later, with a feeding tube in place and weighing in at around 90 pounds, she finally came home.

She was too fragile to touch so, no hugs or cuddles. She looked old and sick and honestly, she rather scared me. From that day forward, her sickness became her identity. Pain pills quickly added to her supply of tranquilizers. Over the next year or so she was barely functional. In came one after another of hired house keepers who would stay with us during the week to keep house and help with care for me and my brother. I didn't like the house keepers and I did not want them to take care of me. I did my best to stay under the radar as much as possible.

We would stay weekends sometimes at Candy Grandma's. She had remarried after divorcing her alcoholic husband of many years to a successful immigrant businessman. Grandpa Sam hailed from Germany, escaping with his sister from a Jewish concentration camp as a young teenager. He had excelled in America as a successful importer/exporter and worked well into his 70s. His harsh exterior coupled with his thick accent had me shy around him. But, he presented me with my first transistor radio which I carried around with me constantly.

I remember Candy Grandma making us oatmeal with half a grapefruit for breakfast. We'd sit out of her sight at her breakfast nook sneaking spoons of sugar when she wasn't looking. *"Stay out of that sugar bowl!"* Candy Grandma had a way of scolding us with love, and I never felt hurt by it. On Sunday mornings after breakfast she would get us ready for church. We would walk the few blocks from her place to the church she attended. Candy Grandma would always be in a dress with her purse matching her high heeled shoes that I can still hear click-clacking down the sidewalk. Afterwards, she would take us to an old fashion diner across the street and let us each order a small bowl of vanilla ice cream. She would drink a cup of coffee, waiting patiently for us to finish. The busy diner with its supply of regular colorful customers always offered great people watching. Such a contrasting atmosphere to our home in the suburbs.

My brother, being a highly spirited child gave my parents a run for their money during this fragile time. He would often stay at Candy Grandma's more often and for longer periods while I stayed at home...so jealous I couldn't go along. If I had only realized that acting up would be my ticket out, I would have raised hell. My nature was quiet, docile...doing what I was told without question. I would escape into my room with my toys and my books becoming obsessed with Are You My Mother? By PD Eastman. As the little bird in the story goes searching for his mother, I identified with him wondering who mine was as well.


Both of my parents were clear from the beginning about our adoptions. I knew I was adopted before I knew what adoption meant. I used to think that it meant I didn't grow and come out of my Mom's tummy and I took great pride in that idea since the thought of it thoroughly disgusted me.

While Mom stayed in the hospital and after our "housekeeper du jour" was finished for the day, nighttime baths and bedtime were Dad's domain.

This was the first time I remember seeing a different side of Dad. Tucked in most nights by him, together we would recite the prayer…

*"Now I lay me down to sleep, I pray the Lord my soul to keep, If I should die before I wake, I pray the Lord my soul to take."*

We'd end with a revolving list of loved ones we prayed for God to bless. He might have been motivated by obligation but, he was tender and caring in these moments and they were wonderful. Even though I was very young, it was clear to me then that he was the more capable parent.

My heart so badly wanted to love and trust him. In rare cases like these, I could give into that need a little and lean on him. As he'd leave my room we would always end with a unison, *"Good night, sleep tight, don't let the bed bugs bite!"* Chaos surrounded us during that time but, in moments like these, Dad stepped up and shared love with his kids. And I am thankful.

Unfortunately, his attention would vanish just as mysteriously as it had appeared. There was a lot of face studying to try to prepare myself for what was to come. I can't begin to imagine how hard that time must have been for both of them. I recall hearing about unannounced visits from social workers to the home to make sure we were being cared for properly.

Mom would be so paranoid that with one bad finding, we'd be taken from them. I was told about an incident a few years earlier at church where their Pastor witnessed Mom being too rough disciplining my brother. Although I had been placed in their home, my adoption was still pending. A report had been filed and an investigation was done. My adoption wasn't final until the winter before my second birthday. This must have made my already anxious mother even worse.

# A Canopy Bed to Boot

We managed somehow to get through the late 60's and even prosper as a result of that terrible time. Mom and Dad sued that quack of a doctor and won. In 1970 they put a down payment on a larger house in a neighboring community. That spring we moved into a beautiful new home. It was a two-story, beige, Mediterranean style, stucco house on a corner lot. Beautiful vaulted ceilings graced the living and dinning rooms with a fancy crystal chandelier hanging in the entryway. New custom furniture, that we were mostly not allowed to sit on, filled each room. And, the best part was, they hired an interior decorator to design mine and my brother's bedrooms! My brother's room had a deep blue nautical theme with a trundle bed and maple furniture that looked like it belonged on a ship. Mine was covered in my favorite shades of green and pink wallpaper — complete with off-white French provincial furniture and a canopy bed to boot! The neighborhood was a newer development with lots of young families yielding plenty of kids to play with. I loved living in that house!

That time carried new energy I believed our whole family could feel with the promise that better days are now ahead.

Mom's body had healed considerably but, she was still not well and in various stages of drug addiction. Dad, when home from work would isolate and stay distant. Thankfully, we had great neighbors that we spent lots of time with. Looking back, I think they could sense that my brother and I needed a little extra help. Thank God for the Meeker's the Keller's, the Smith's, the Mckinzie's…people from the church.

We didn't go as a family but, Mom and Dad wanted us to be exposed to the gospel so, they found a good Baptist church nearby and would drop us off on Sunday mornings. A middle-aged couple ministered the church. The husband would do the preaching, and the wife taught our Sunday school classes. We spent some time with them outside of church and I was surprised by how different they were than my parents with their positivity and smiles. All in all we had some pretty amazing people who were there for us and, we are better because of their involvement.

My love affair with music started during this time. Dad strictly forbade us to listen to rock and roll, certain that it would send us astray. This however, didn't stop us from sneaking. My Vans tennis shoes and I would peddle around the neighborhood on my Schwinn bike with my little transistor radio from Grandpa Sam dangling from the handlebars with it's colorful streamers flying in the wind. Elton John, Three Dog Night, The Jackson 5, The Carpenters, Olivia Newton John, James Taylor, Stevie Wonder... I knew every word to every song.

Weekend hiking adventures in the California foothills with friend's families were such great escapes and an opportunity to be myself and accepted for who I was. Those close to our family knew my brother and I were adopted. Others would constantly comment how I didn't look like any of them. My dark brown hair, freckles and brown eyes definitely had me looking like I came from a different tribe. When I was a baby, our hispanic neighbor lady would call me her *"little Juanita."* Mom would correct her every time. *"Her name is Barbara!"* Whenever Mom dropped me off at school, kids would ask, *"Is that your real Mom?"* My friends who knew I was adopted would often ask me about my birth-Mom... *"Why didn't she keep you?"* *"Don't you want to find her?"* My reaction would surprise them, as I seemed indifferent in regards to her. Instead, I was very curious about my birth-Dad. She chose to give me up...my birth-Dad might not have if he knew about me, or at least that's how I made sense of things. With Dad consistently showing disinterest in me, I'd dream up scenarios where my birth-Dad would undoubtedly find me irresistible and worth his time and attention. I had to protect myself from the true story of my existence from the very beginning. My independent streak came early out of necessity.

I had learned early on to keep a very low profile, performing obediently and dancing around Mom's constantly changing behavior. Angering her could yield a multitude of reactions. The stupidest thing would send her into a rage to run from. Her form of discipline was the complete opposite of Dad's. She would quickly lash out with slaps that would sting, sometimes reaching for the nearest object to throw or hit us with.

Our home had a three car garage and in the third unused stall, we had a ping-pong table set up. On a late fall chilly afternoon, I was outside playing, wearing a lightweight waist-length jacket. Mom was doing laundry in the garage when we started playing ping-pong. I was doing my best to hold my own against my brother who seemed to do everything better than me and as I wielded my paddle, my jacket would fall down off my shoulders and hang at my mid-back onto my forearms. Mom was in one of her moods and told me to pull my jacket back up onto my shoulders. Again, with eager playing making me warm, it would fall back down. For some unknown reason, this angered Mom beyond reason. She would scream with exaggeration to pull my jacket back up. To which to appease her, I would, again… It must have been the third or fourth time that my jacket fell down that did it for her. Without warning, she grabbed a fiberglass fishing rod that happened to be hanging on the garage wall and began frantically hitting me with it. My jacket was just thick enough to protect my upper body from the strikes that the fishing rod delivered but, there was a weighted lure connected to the rod that hit me in my lower stomach below my belly button. The pain was searing! With her compromised condition, it wasn't too difficult to run from her, which I did as fast as I could. My feelings would be so shattered with these actions. I never intended to anger her… I just wanted to play ping pong.

A few days later while getting dressed in my bedroom, I saw a huge, black and purple bruise forming. It covered a much larger area than the lure had hit, extending the whole area of my lower stomach. I could hear my brother in the hallway and told him to come into my room. I showed him the bruise and he went ballistic! Quickly running into Mom's room, screaming at her.

*"You should see what you did to her!! She has a huge bruise because of you!!!"*

Startled, Mom came into my room and insisted I show her. She looked quite shocked but, I could detect a little bit of relief in her eyes when she saw the location, knowing it would not be seen by anyone else.

So often I could feel the anger radiating off of her. She would respond 10 times stronger than a situation warranted, always taking offenses ultra personal. Mom knew how to use her words to cause great harm. Her tone and expression would frighten me so, making trusting her impossible. She was good at storing up her grievances and hurling them at me when she snapped.

I shared very little of myself with her. Only the version she wanted to see.

Mom would flip from a monster to a sad little girl, to a brooding teenager and then to a kind reasonable person in the snap of a finger. Her unpredictability was the only predictable thing about her. Later, after her rage cooled, came her apology. Which would come to mean nothing.

After school one day, I went outside to find something to do. It was common in our neighborhood to show up at each other's doorstep to hang out, ride bikes…This particular day, a neighbor girl who was a couple of years older than me had just gotten a brand new bike. The other neighbor girls were taking turns riding it and I wanted to join in on the fun. I stepped forward to ask for a turn — to which the owner of the new bike harshly told me *"No!"* and to *"Go Home!"*

For some reason without missing a beat I leaned forward and screamed a huge *"FUCK YOU!!!"* In their direction — to which received and immediate collective gasp with huge eyes and open mouths. The girls quickly announced that they were telling my mother! I couldn't have it! Mom would do God-only-knows-what to me for saying THAT! I had never uttered the word before in my life and to this day, I have no idea why it came out of my mouth. I spun on my heels and raced home in a panic with the girls right behind me.

Mom happened to be close to the door when I barged in running straight up to my room. *"What's wrong?"* She asked. Ding Dong — there goes the doorbell. I barely get to my room as I hear the girls at the door. *"Mrs. Reddick, we came to tell you what your daughter said!"* I close my door not able to handle what they're saying. Finally the front door shuts. There I sit waiting for the bomb to drop.

More time went by than I expected and eventually Mom saunters upstairs and comes into my room. I am scared to death. She's very composed and quietly asks, *"Did you say what they said you did?"* No words...head down nodding yes. *"That's a very bad word."* She tells me. *"I know."* She goes on, *"You know you should never say it again."* I reply shaking my head.

*"I won't. I promise...sorry Mom."* Tears. At this, she turned and left the room. That was it! We never spoke about it again. I was in utter amazement. Still am.

# If It Weren't For You...

Our family was split down the middle. Mom picked me to be her reluctant teammate. Her control of me was constant. Every moment of every day was a performance to keep her happy. If I behaved just right, she would delight and I was her buddy. She would discuss things with me like I was a 40-year- old woman expected to understand what I was not able to, including details about her and Dad's sex life and her dissatisfaction with it's infrequency.

Sometimes she would indulge me in buying me pretty things I admired. Including a pair of white, zip up, go-go boots. She tried to talk me into getting the boring brown ones, worried white would never stay white, but I lobbied hard and she reluctantly gave in. I wore those boots practically every day until they didn't fit anymore, and I'm pretty sure they didn't stay white. We'd make trips to the sewing store where she would pick out fabric and patterns that she would make into dresses and outfits for me. I would pretend to like them because she was so proud to have made them. If I didn't pretend enough, the risk of her spinning into a rage was great. I appreciated her efforts to sew me clothing, I just wished she would have consulted with me about what I might like. We couldn't have had more opposite taste.

A couple of times a year she would sit me down in the middle of the kitchen to perm my hair. *"We have to get rid of that awful straight hair of yours!"* I liked my straight hair and wanted to look like the other girls my age. I remember the first day of second grade, excited to be back at school to see my friends. Out on the playground, Mark Swanson came running up to greet me but, then stoped suddenly looking shocked! *"What happened to your hair?!"* Days earlier Mom had given me an Olgivie home perm with pink rods...THAT'S what happened!

Mom's constant need for attention was next to impossible to fulfill and yet, I did my best to which when successful, put me in her good graces. It was very important to stay there because the alternative was terrorizing. If I didn't show exuberant appreciation for Mom's jesters, the energy would shift and I would be punished for thinking things I was not at all thinking. I became a master at reading people. It was paramount to living in peace as best as I could.

I wanted to love her so badly. I would search for tiny glimpses of light from her that I could grab onto. Occasionally, a spark would fly and I would give her my all. Dad so consistently pushed me away. He could do it with a look. I was not the daughter he was hoping for and hardly a day went by that he didn't let me know it. I tried so hard to make myself invisible to him…insignificant, quiet. Hoping somehow by doing so that I could meet his standards and earn his love. I needed Mom to love me. As long as I performed perfectly, she gave love as she could. And, I received it. By around age eight she was frequently telling me that I was the only reason she didn't throw a noose over the upstairs railing and end it all. I must have heard her say, *"If it weren't for you …"* hundreds of times. I felt so responsible for her being ok and took my role seriously — never arguing with her and always doing as I was told.

Dad and she frequently fought about her condition and the drugs. On occasion he would scour the house ridding it of all the pain pills and tranquilizers. After one of his purges, she packed up the car with suitcases filled with our clothes, various household items and her sewing machine, that she was certain she could make a living with. People didn't send their clothes out for mending so much anymore but, she was convinced it was her ticket to independence. Mom gave me no option other than to go with her… *"I couldn't bear to live without you." "You'll only fight with your brother." "Don't think your Dad wants you here!"* — were some of her arguments. Mom did what she could to consistently put Dad in a bad light. Her efforts did not make me despise him. Instead, they made me think even less of her.

The car was packed full and it was time to leave. Dad had my brother outside helping him trouble shoot a flaw with the sprinkler system when we pulled out of the driveway. Mom rolled the window down and told them they would never see us again. Dad said nothing making no eye contact in our direction. As the car pulled out of the driveway and onto the street, I stared at his face with the late afternoon sun shining on his profile. Waiting, hoping he would look at me. Tell me I don't have to go. Please tell me you want me to stay.

He did not. Instead he stared off with no expression. This confirmed Mom's argument. I honestly don't think he had the strength to fight with her, but to my tender young heart, that rejection was devastating.

The first few days on the road were quite chaotic. Mom clearly had no plan, and the uncertainty of where we would land made me stressed and confused. Mom did however allow me to take control over the radio and I could choose whatever station I wanted. *"Don't tell your Dad or brother!"* Wait, what?! I thought we were never going to see them again. My beloved transistor radio songs sounded amazing on car stereo speakers! Mom made attempts to stay with some of her relatives but, that would burn out pretty quickly. We stayed at hotels with pools until the credit card ran dry. I spent my days swimming instead of going to school. Eventually, she would drag us back home with her tail between her legs. Having no discussion with Dad, we would all just carry on like nothing ever happened. With these excursions, Dad would get even more distant with me showing disproval and anger over anything I did or said. For him, I could not perform and gain his love.

Dad would make me sit down and practice for hours writing words out in effort to cure my backwards b's and d's. When it was time to learn math, his electrical engineer brain couldn't comprehend that my dominant right brain struggled so. Was it 47 or 74? 81 or 18? My eyes and brain were seeing different things. In these attempts to teach me, he would lack patience and out of frustration, treat me like I was terribly stupid. This would anger Mom and widen the divide between them. In second grade, Dad wanted me to be tested to see what was wrong and why learning certain subjects was so challenging for me. I remember staying up really late one night so I would be tired the next day. We went for testing at a facility housed in a large building in Los Angeles. I was put in a room alone and told to draw pictures while I was observed behind two-way glass. Then, electrodes were glued to my scalp and my brain waves were studied while I slept. I felt really insecure about all this testing and asked my Dad... *"Are they testing me because they think I'm retarded?"* (A term widely used in the 70's.) Dad's expression read cold and he casually answered, *"Something like that."* His cold affect did nothing to rescue my insecurities. Instead, I have spent a lifetime trying to prove to everyone that I am not stupid.

Ultimately, the diagnosis was Dyslexia, which I was predicted to outgrow in time. I was not made aware of this diagnosis until years later. Why this information was kept from me, I'll never understand. It's almost as if he didn't want me to know that I was normal and would be ok.

# I Choose Glen Campbell

From time to time, Mom would enter into the hospital for various reasons that I honestly don't remember. Possibly stemming from her medical accident, and procedures following or, it could be to sober up — which she did off and on throughout the years. When Mom was not at home, Dad would occasionally allow his other side to again show. During one of Mom's absences, a particular Saturday remains firm in my memory. I was nine years old. My brother was away for the weekend with friends. Dad asked me if I wanted to take a ride with him as he was shopping for a new camera. Someone had put an add in the paper selling their gently used high quality camera, a type Dad was interested in. So excited, I got ready...even putting on a dress which he always preferred.

I fixed my hair and then we drove the hour or so distance to take a look. He was fun and lighthearted in the car. He cracked jokes with me and we stoped for snacks. With Dad, rock and roll was strictly forbidden but ironically, country music was ok. Looking through the console's available 8-tracks, he let me choose... Roger Miller or Glen Campbell?

I chose Glen Campbell and to this day whenever I hear his songs, I'm back in that car with my Dad. When we arrived to the seller's house, he was demonstrating the camera out in his garage and offered to take our picture. I'm glad Dad decided to purchase that camera because this photo came home with us. All these years latter when I look at this picture, I'm reminded of this day.

This day, I had the Dad I wanted. The smiling Dad. The Dad who saw me and acknowledged me. On the way home we listened to the new song on country radio called "The Streak" and I was ecstatic to have my otherwise stoic, uptight Dad laughing hysterically with me.

The Dad who tucked me in and said prayers was back. This day was proof of what could be possible and I was filled with hope. Once Mom was back in the house, the dynamic would shift back to what we were all familiar with. Dad's back turned to me once again. The smiling and laughter, gone. The eye contact and talking were no more. But, this day! It was wonderful…and I cherish it still.

Dad and I

Growing up in Norman and Marion's home was very confusing. Christmas and birthdays were made special. We received nice gifts and they enjoyed giving them. When Mom was sober, she would pack up the station wagon with sandwiches, cookies, and drinks... tell us to call our friends and we'd all spend the day at the beach. It was as if Mom and Dad knew what kind of parents they wanted to be and at times, would make great gestures. I always craved consistency and would do all I could to support it. But, we never seemed to stay steady for long.

Most of Mom's family now lived in Southern California and would sometimes come over to our house for holidays or to visit. They were warm and loving...and so funny! Candy Grandma, my aunts, uncles, and cousins would fill our house with life. Laughter would echo with those high ceilings. But when they left, all of that energy would go right out the door with them. Solitude and quiet would takes its place again leaving little opportunity for laughter or life.

By 1975, Dad was self-employed. He left the security that the corporate world offered and carved out a new career for himself. This involved driving out to rural areas calling on dairy farmers and offering them savings through consolidating their energy bills. Given this resulted in a one time service appointment, Dad had to cover more and more territory driving further north and it kept him from being at home. This gave opportunity for Mom to do as she pleased. The situation was headed to implode and something had to change.

# Demons in Our Closet...

The beautiful house was sold. Those goodbyes were devastating knowing we were leaving a community that sheltered us. No more hikes in the foothills. No more Sunday school. No more visits with Candy Grandma. We relocated to central California to be nearer to agricultural areas. Gone were the vaulted ceilings and custom painted rooms. Instead, we moved into a one level, smaller home more suited to Mom's difficulty with breathing due to damage from Dr. Quack. I entered sixth grade in a new school and my brother entered eighth.

My relationship with my brother is filled with memories of arguments and arm punches. My earliest memories of him come around three or four years old. He would wake me up early on Saturday mornings to go into the living room and watch cartoons. Mom and Dad would't be up yet. It was often still dark out and with the console TV turned on, the white snowy pre programing screen would illuminate the room. He would lay on the sofa and make me sit on his feet, complaining that they were cold. Usually, he would fall asleep while I sat there uncomfortably keeping his feet warm and wondering, why aren't we still in bed? I loved cartoons as much as most kids but, he could not wait for the high energy colorful images to fill his Saturday mornings. This kid could make me laugh harder than anyone. His hyper silliness would assist when mimicking our parents. He and I would share sideways looks over inside jokes that if picked up on, we'd get punished over.

As we got older, we fought with each other A LOT! Dad often pulled ideas out of his military training. Usually, we were disciplined by being "restricted" from each other. Honestly, I don't think either of us minded. It was a needed break from one another. He hung out with his friends and I with mine. He belonged to Dad and I belonged to Mom. My brother had more energy and intelligence than anyone in the household. That energy often got him into trouble. He almost always got caught for breaking the rules and he definitely pushed the limits. I dodged a lot of bullets making sure not to follow in his footsteps. At this point in time, my brother was smoking cigarettes and occasionally sneaking out of his room at night. But, what a master he was at sneaking the forbidden music into the house. He had great hiding places. We both had TVs and stereos in our rooms and spent a fair amount of time hiding out. I was more of a Captain and Tennille, Bay City Rollers kind of girl, but my brother introduced me to some really different stuff. Supertramp, Sweet, Kansas, Boston, Forigner, Aerosmith, Kiss, and the infamous Frampton Comes Alive to name a few. On rare occasions, Mom and Dad would take off together. Visits with Dr.'s discussing possible treatments for all of Mom's issues could have them gone for hours. My brother's room had a perfect view of our driveway. We would hang out there playing music at max volume, rocking out and lip syncing to Ballroom Blitz followed by as much music as we could play before they came home. Air guitaring and singing along…pouring over the album covers and relating to the lyrics in an almost scary way. When Supertramp told us we had *"Demons in our closet and we're screaming out to stop it…"* WOW! How did THEY know?!!

Listening to this music was like ice to a burn. Such a necessary escape for us, and we connected over it, taking refuge and building strength so we could continue on. Taking turns, we would constantly be checking the window. As soon as we detected the car's return, we'd get everything put away and hidden before they walked in the door. We never got busted! If Dad did find my brother's music, he'd destroy it. A bit of a problem when those albums and tapes were borrowed.

As much as we annoyed one another, my brother and I could come together for the sake of powering through this experience we were living out in this family. When necessary, he would rise up to protect me. Back when I started kindergarten we would walk to school together but, I walked home alone at the lunch hour. There were a couple of older neighborhood boys that would harass me…push me behind the fence and tell me to lift up my dress. I would cry and cry shouting *"NO!"* But, they would corner me and tell me to do it or

I couldn't go home. Eventually I'd break away and run like crazy with them chasing close behind me. This happened more than once. One day my brother was home sick from school. I ran through the door in tears. He asked me why I was crying and I told him. As he went out to look, those two boys took off running. There goes my seven-year-old brother running full speed in his pajamas chasing those boys all the way down the street. He could beat the crap out of me and call me every bad name he could think of but, don't mess with his sister.

As I matured and entered into puberty, along with growing taller, my middle also grew bigger. Having such sweet snacks at our fingertips was too tempting to pass up. Mom always had the pantry and freezer stocked with foods of convenience. That often meant snacks with Hostess and Dolly Madison on the label. My weight increased but, somehow, I was rather oblivious to it. Apparently I was focused on other things. Preteen things. Spending as much time as I could away from home hanging out with my friends, listening to music, pouring over the latest issue of Tiger Beat magazine, and of course, talking about all the boys we had crushes on.

I was always so envious of the relationships my friends had with their Dads. Seeing the impromptu hugs, acting silly with each other and witnessing just the right amount of teasing… The day in the car, camera shopping with Dad was the only time I can remember having any semblance of that. Our home environment didn't welcome ease of company with each other. So, it made more sense to shrink away and not engage.

One day during the summer I turned twelve, I rode my bike home from a friend's pool where we had swam most of the day. Wearing my one piece swimsuit with my towel around my neck, I jumped off my bike and came inside making a B-line to the kitchen sink where I filled up a glass and chugged water…so thirsty…another glass. All of the sudden, I see Dad out of the corner of my eye watching me. As I look at him, I see his eyes go up and down looking at my chubby swimsuit body standing there.

*"We have GOT to do something about reducing your weight!"*

His words hit me hard. A giant wave of shame covered my whole body and I could hardly breathe. The already fragile relationship we had, felt like it shattered into a million more painful cuts. He didn't elaborate any further. Instead, he just walked away with a look of disgust. His words and expression mixed with a lifetime of pushing me away delivered a message that day that bypassed my brain and shot straight into my heart's core.

It was in that moment I learned…Men will always find me undesirable. Repulsive. Worthless. I believed it.

I've tried very hard over the years to reason it away but, It has never left me. Things shifted for me that summer and I slowly began to turn even further away from him — expecting nothing. I no longer allowed myself to put any trust in him — the "more capable" parent. Instead, I realized that with all of Mom's issues coupled with his rejection, I can only rely on myself. I'm on a solo mission to get myself to safety and far away from their wake.

# Losing Ground

The drug patterns with Mom continued to cycle. Dad was putting more pressure on her which never yielded the results he was after. Mom packed everything up and announced that we were moving out. Again. This time she found us a crappy, cheap, furnished apartment on the other side of town. This required me to change schools. I had just started seventh grade at Jr. High where at least my friends from sixth grade were in my classes. At this school, I knew no one and the kids seemed rougher. Mom was using so heavily that I was completely on my own to do everything — get myself to school, prepare meals, do my homework, and make sure she was ok. I would come back to the apartment from school some days and find her comatose. Witnessing her in that condition again and again broke something in me. We never discussed her drug use. Never. Somehow I knew if I said one word, that it would end the little bit of stability I had. There were no visits with Dad. No phone calls. Mom dragged me with her into her darkness and there we both sat…day after day. Where was I to go? With Mom's strong personality, her family wouldn't dare go up against her. She wasn't someone you challenged. Dad certainly wasn't going to save me. My only choice was to play along, hide my thoughts and feelings and wait.

I can't quite remember how long we lived in that apartment. I'm pretty sure Candy Grandma was funding it and I'm guessing that those funds came to an end. One day I came home to find Mom in the middle of packing up again. She decided we were moving back to Southern California. We went to stay with old next-door-neighbors from the house we lived in when I was little. I'm curious how many people must have told her "No" before she scrounged up old neighbors that we had not had any interaction with in several years. This family was lovely and sincere — even driving up to help us move. We stayed at their house for a few weeks. Mom's heavy drug use continued. Eventually, they had witnessed enough and we had to leave. Back to the hotels with pools. I did not go to school. I didn't even go swimming. I just took care of Mom. She relied on me for everything. I was her caretaker, her buddy, her life line and her emotional punching bag. After some time we got a note from the front desk under our door. Mom packed up the car and off we went. While driving, Mom started to go comatose. I could see her slipping and I kept yelling at her… *"Mom! Mom!!"* The car would veer into traffic and then go the opposite way and hit the guard rail. I tried hanging onto the steering wheel to keep it straight. We'd speed up and then slow way down. The things that stick with you… Blinded By The Light, by Manfred Mann's Earth Band was playing on the radio during this whole ordeal. We finally crashed into something that brought the car to a stop. Bystanders started coming by to offer aid. Mom was non-responsive.

A man came up to the drivers side of the car. He was in his mid-thirties with dark blond hair and bright blue eyes. He looked rather trustworthy. Help and concern shown on his face. He convinced me to roll down the window. Somehow, he seemed to understand what was happening with Mom and he spoke kindly to me while putting the car in park and removing the keys. Soon I heard sirens. Fire and police showed up with an ambulance. They got Mom out of the car and put her on a stretcher. The EMT's questions made it obvious they suspected drinking, but I quickly corrected them and then rattled off the names of all the drugs she took. The list was a long one and the looks on their faces convinced me that this was not normal. I rode along in the ambulance and we headed to the nearest hospital. The nice man stayed until we left. I wish I would've thanked him. I wasn't sure exactly where we were but I knew it wasn't far from the old neighborhood. Once we entered the ER and they began to evaluate Mom, I went into survival mode. Walking the halls, I found a pay phone and immediately called my friend Bridget Mckinzie from our old neighborhood. She put her Mom on the phone and I told her what had happened. The next thing I know, Bridget and her Dad came to the hospital and picked me up! I left without saying a word to anyone. Spending the next few days at Bridget's house was pure bliss. Playing records and dancing around Bridget's room, going to the mall and playing air hockey, having dinners with her family and feeling safe. I honestly would have been happy to stay there forever. One afternoon, someone rang their doorbell. Her Dad went to answer the door and it was our former Pastor from our old little Baptist church Mom and Dad used to drop us off at when we were kids. My old Pastor kindly told me he was there to take me to see my mother. How did she find me? I so badly wanted to say... *"No! Please let me stay here!!"* But, instead, I said nothing. I got my things together and left with him.

# Wisconsin Blues

We only lasted in central California for just over two years. Apparently, Dad cycled through all the available dairy farms within driving distance and decided, what better place to embark on than the dairy capital of the world? We moved as a family this time to central Wisconsin. More goodbyes... This time, most of the custom furniture was sold along with just about everything else. Late summer of 1977 we landed in a tiny town of less than 400 people. I'm not sure how long it took, but eventually Dad learned that most of the dairy farms in the area belonged to a co-op that already provided what he was selling. Here we were, transplanted from California to the middle-of-nowhere, Wisconsin with no work opportunities for Dad. Mom, my brother and I stayed in Wisconsin while Dad traveled back to California to continue to generate income. Or at least, that's what we were told at the time.

My brother and I did not embrace Midwest small town living very well. We joked that all the people looked the same, and everyone wore glasses! Does living in Wisconsin somehow give you bad eyesight? At school we thought the kids were so unsophisticated. My brother and I spent time at the local small town diner and would gorge ourselves on hamburgers and French fries. My brother, with a pocket full of quarters would play all the singles from Hotel California on the jukebox over and over again. I think those waitresses wanted to murder us!

I missed California terribly and everything that was left behind. My friends and their safe families, the warm sunshine, the shear vibe of home. It was in Wisconsin that I began writing. I would fill up notebook after notebook with white lined paper and there I'd put down all my thoughts and feelings. All my frustrations and anger. My hatred. These things were never talked about out loud to anyone. I continued writing until my early twenties. Several years later, sadly all those notebooks would be destroyed in a house fire.

After eight long months in Wisconsin, Mom decided we needed to head to an area that yielded more job opportunities for Dad. We moved one state over to the west and settled in the Twin Cities. Mom found our family of four a new home in a crowded low-income townhome rental complex where most of our neighbors we were instructed to avoid. Dad drove back from California and met us there.

I started 9th grade at a high school where all the kids had been together since kindergarten. A very tough crowd to break into. Being the new kid, along with carrying more weight around than the average skinny girls my age made me an easy target. As I walked down the halls, some of the boys would throw themselves up against the lockers, exaggerating making room for me to walk by. *"Make way! Wide load!!"* They'd laugh with each other while I walked by as quickly as possible keeping my head down. I can still hear the sound of them crashing against the lockers. Sharing these occurrences with Mom, her remedy was to stay home and keep her company. Much like the times when she left Dad and needed me around. I missed a lot of school in my freshman year which made assimilating that much more difficult. I managed to make a couple of new friends but, largely stayed to myself. I wasn't a brain. I wasn't a jock, or a burnout. I honestly could not see where I might fit in. At home, I hung out in my room as much as possible...listening to the forbidden music with headphones on and writing in my journals. Dreaming of my escape.

By now, I was so accustomed to living in this family where I did not belong. I was not known...so certain my true self would not yield love in this home. The two things I learned to do very well was, perform and hide.

Halfway through ninth grade we moved a few miles away and rented the larger half of a duplex just a couple of blocks from my school. Mom was always looking for opportunities to "level up" in regards to our living conditions. I appreciated that in her. Sadly, since leaving the beautiful corner house in California with the vaulted ceilings, I believed our best days as a family were behind us.

Not long after our move, law enforcement from Wisconsin came calling. Dad was served a subpoena, forcing him to return to Wisconsin to face charges of mail fraud. Apparently, in the early months living in Wisconsin, Dad sold several accounts to a number of dairy farmers and charged them for his services that he was not able to provide due to the state co-op they all belonged to. Dad knowingly misled these farmers and when they became aware of it, he high-tailed it back to California.

He now had to face a jury trial out of Medford, Wisconsin. Dad was ultimately found guilty and sentenced to serve three months time in a minimum security prison in Minnesota. I have no idea how we made ends meet during that time. I suspect Candy Grandma came to the rescue once again. My brother and I wrote letters to him but, there were no visits. He told Mom he didn't want us to see him there. I know this experience took a huge toll on my Dad and I remember feeling sorry for him but also, I was hugely disappointed in my most "capable" parent. Once he was back home, Dad tried a few sales jobs…selling mobile homes and even burial plots but, not very successfully. His sentence and time served were never talked about, as if it had never happened. Our family's income was at an all time low. We even went on public assistance for a time and drank powdered milk. After neglecting to make payments, one of our vehicles got repossessed.

Mom pressured Dad and insisted he go back to work as an electrical engineer. He pushed back claiming his agoraphobia made working in the corporate world nearly impossible. But, Mom having the stronger personality won out and eventually, Dad was fortunate enough to go to work "under contract" for 3M, who's huge corporate office was just a couple of miles away.

# Action!

In late winter of my junior year, notices were posted around campus announcing tryouts for the school spring play, The Mousetrap. Somehow, it called out to me and for some reason I knew that I had to try out. I gave a pretty convincing pitch to Mom and she signed my permission slip without any argument. Out of nowhere, my shyness was replaced with courage. I showed up at the audition and when it was my turn, followed the director's orders and acted out what she asked...

Read from the script alone, and with others. Did some improving as a news anchor and even gave a mediocre weather forecast.

I would have been thrilled to be involved in any capacity, but to be in the play! What a dream...

A few days later, the play was cast. I walked up to the theater doors where the posted names were hung, and as read down the list I saw...

Miss Casewell will be played by............ Barb Reddick

It was like I was hit by lightning!! In a good way! A lead part! My thoughts soared and my heart sailed all at the same time. Somehow, I was certain I could do this. I didn't know how I knew, but nonetheless, I knew without a doubt! I flew home from school that day on a cloud. I don't think my feet touched the ground at all. My dream had come true and the electricity running through me was palpable. But, as I arrived home, I quietly downplayed the news knowing if I showed my excitement, somehow Mom would ruin it for me.

Mom and Dad had very little in common but, one conviction they both carried was, zero tolerance for any semblance of pride. To them, pride equaled conceit. God forbid you would be proud of yourself for any accomplishment because you would be knocked down and put in your place immediately. I remember my brother winning a DECA award in high school. He was so proud of it and couldn't wait to come home and show our parents. Upon looking at it, Mom rolled off a snide *"Well, look at you! You think you're really something, don't you?"* To which my brother hurled his award across the room.

The next several weeks were busy with rehearsals. We learned our lines and worked on stage blocking. There were no personal microphones back then so we had to really work on voice projection. We did everything...built and painted our sets. Scrounged for stage furniture and wardrobe. The long rehearsal hours after school gave me a reason to be away from home and I was on top of the world.

After several weeks of hard work, we put on two separate performances over a weekend. The lights, the full auditorium, the buzz... There was something special in the air, and it was life-giving! Mom came to see the play by herself. When I saw her sitting in the audience, she was chatting it up with strangers. I knew her monologue so well. Everyone she met would hear about her medical accident and the 32 operations....

Midwesterners were often mortified hearing the story which was the reaction she liked best. With all of that aside, I could tell that she was very proud. It was weeks later that Dad admitted he came in and sat in the back to watch. I was too afraid to ask him what he thought because I didn't want to hear. He was rather free with his criticism and very sparse with his praise.

As the school year continued, I had become a little bit more known and things started opening up to me. The new found confidence I carried was serving me well.

# Regret

September 1981 was the start of my senior year. It wasn't long before the fall school play auditions were announced. This time it was The Diary of Ann Frank, — a bit more of a challenge than our light hearted Agatha Christie play the previous spring. I auditioned and got the part of Mrs. Van Daan. So exciting! I took my roll very seriously doing my best self-absorbed, middle-aged woman on lockdown. Again, there were two performances over a weekend. Both shows were sold out and our review in the school paper was raving. Once again, Mom came to see the play alone. Like before, it was a huge high for me...this time, maybe even more. I was connected to something bright and wonderful and I belonged there. Dad didn't mention he had seen the play so, I assumed he did not go. As winter passed, I knew it wouldn't be long until the spring play would be announced. — Not that I was a tad focused on it, mind you. I had found my niche...something I was good at and I recognized it in the eyes of others.

Dad asked me if I was trying out, and I said I was.

It was then that he admitted that he had come to see The Diary of Ann Frank. I asked him if he liked it. Big mistake!

*"I thought it was much too heavy of a subject matter for a high school play."*

He answered quickly, like he had been sitting on his comment eagerly waiting to offer its cold effect. Nothing else was said, which added to the weight of it hanging in the air.

I had spent the the last few years shutting him out — with great success I might say — not relying on him for anything and graduating from hate to a place of indifference. Why did I even ask? More importantly, why did his opinion weigh so much that I struggled to catch my breath? My joy and excitement was wiped out by a single sentence I should never have solicited.

I did not try out for the spring play. I did however go see it on opening night and immediately noticed the part that was supposed to be mine. The girl who had it, instead of me did a decent job, but I missed out on all the weeks of rehearsals. The set building, the camaraderie and fun we had as a group. Learning my lines and practically everyone els's. The anticipation of opening night. The rush of being on stage. I missed out on it all. Self-loathing and self sabotage were now directing me. I agreed with the idea that I wasn't worthy of the experience. It was a huge mistake and I've regretted it ever since.

My brother was now smoking pot with friends and behaving more combative with Mom and Dad. Going through his pockets while doing laundry, Mom found notes between friends detailing pot smoking. Sharing this with Dad of course created quite the storm. I recall going as a family to a drug rehab center where we met with a counselor. I'm pretty sure we only went one time, as my parents did not like hearing this notion that they played a part in it all. The situation continued and ramped up to an unfortunate outcome. Mom and Dad found pot or, at least strong evidence of it in the house. Dad enraged, unleashed anger in a way I'd never witnessed before. His mild manner vanished. Yelling turned into screaming, and eventually things got violent between them. Dad put my brother in some sort of hold… I'm assuming a fast move he learned in his Marine Corps training. Once he was released, my brother punched a huge hole in the sheet rock, amidst Dad screaming at the top of his lungs, *"I WILL NOT HAVE DRUGS IN THIS HOUSE!!!"*

I think we could all choke on the irony. My brother was kicked out of the house that day and never moved back. He left with his clothes stuffed inside his Mustang Cobra 2. I loved that car — took my drivers test with it. I'm pretty sure he slept in it for a while before he landed somewhere. Soon after, he met his future wife. A sweet, smart, lovely girl with long, blond hair and kind, brown eyes. They were both 18 when they met and were married a year later. She had a typical large Minnesota family that embraced and loved him unconditionally, and they still do. Watching him as he ran away, part of me left with him. But I understood, and was so happy for him. He found his refuge.

Mom and Dad ignored each other as much as possible. They both seemed to be as miserable as two people could possibly be. I couldn't understand why they stayed together. Their depiction of marriage was enough to make one wonder, why would anyone do this to themselves? Once my brother was out of the house, Mom became even needier. Spending my time with her was the only life or outlet Mom had and she constantly made me aware of it. If I wanted to spend time with friends, she'd pout and I'd feel guilty. She no longer could get away with the excessive drug use living under the same roof as Dad and, by now she seemed to somewhat accept that. Her using became less frequent yet, her behavior didn't change much. There was still the outbursts over nothing, the false accusations over what I was thinking about her, and the need to carefully walk on those eggshells.

All I could think about was escaping. Darkness had now settled in to stay. Reading about suicide, I imagined the relief it would bring. The thought didn't scare or repulse me. It actually drew me in and I fantasized about it daily.

# Drifting

As senior year wrapped up, my teachers were asking me where I planned to go to college. College!? The subject was never brought up at home. There was no talk in our household about what would come next after graduation. On my own, I had no idea how to even go about looking into it. Neither Mom or Dad ever asked what interested me. Nor told me what they noticed I was good at. I honestly don't think they had any idea. At my graduation ceremony on the football field of our school, toilet paper streamers and colorful beach balls were tossed around between us while speeches were made and diplomas handed out. The excitement in the air was not shared with me. Afterwards, families joined us on the field where hugs were given and pictures were taken. Some of my friend's parents shared a hug and congratulated me. Mom and my brother's new bride sat in the bleachers but, did not come down. Dad experienced it parked next to the field sitting in his car with the windows down. We didn't go out for dinner. There was no cake...no party. After turning in my cap and gown, I walked home by myself...diploma in hand. I was not excited about my future. Instead, I was at a complete loss with no vision. With high school now out of the way, my identity crisis was standing toe to toe with me, staring me straight in the eye. Who am I? What am I? How do I change this direction I'm drifting? What did change after graduation was the fact that I now had to pay for room and board. To start, the fee was $150 every month. Dad assuring me that I'd never be able to live that cheap anywhere, and I knew he was right.

After a few months of baby sitting for the neighbors, a friend got me a job where she worked. 3M's large corporation contained several separate buildings on its large campus — many of them having large cafeterias offering lunch to the numerous employees spending their days there. I would arrive early in the morning to help prepare the lunch options available daily. The menus rotated regularly and it was quite the operation. The job came with decent benefits and stock options. The hourly pay wasn't bad but the best part was, my co-workers — mostly all women old enough to be my Mom. They were a bunch of canny Norwegian gals who taught me a lot and I adored them. During prep and clean up I learned how to measure and weigh food portions, make metal steam trays shine and balance out a cash register. The jokes would fly among them and I witnessed what hard work really looked like.

By age 19 I also worked part time evenings and weekends at a local Ground Round as a hostess. Showing up to work all dressed up in cute outfits, hair done and makeup on as I showed people to their tables. This was my fun job and the people I worked with were young and loved to party! It was while working here that my social life really took flight. Some of the girls my age introduced me to night clubs where we would drink in excess and dance for hours. I went to work parties where I learned how to do tequila shots and snorted my first line of cocaine. Amazing new music would be played and I learned about this new local artist named Prince. These people were kind of like a family. A common response to working lots of hours with each other, often in stressful dinner rushes with the end result of a successful night being quite the bonding experience. After close, we often gathered around the bar for a celebratory drink or 2, or 3…

I felt rather accepted and known there. Friendships were established and I was learning how to have fun.

Working both jobs, I became focused on making enough money to move out. The other advantage of working two jobs was that I was rarely around to be subject to the discord raging at home. I was up early and off to my 3M job. After lunch service, much cleaning would need to be done to get ready for the next day. I would get home around 3pm, change clothes and head to the Ground Round where I would often close. Usually arriving home after Mom and Dad had gone to bed.

The 3M employees I served lunch to were so good to me. After getting to know some of them, I was offered a night job to come into the office in the evenings to do computer back-up. It would be much easier than working at the restaurant. Only a couple of hours a night with less standing. I hated to have to say goodby to the party people but, this could possibly lead to a "real job." Something to build on leading to a paycheck that could fulfill a dream away from Mom and Dad.

# Who Poured
# Red Paint All Over Me?

I came into the office after work for a couple of weeks to receive some extra training and finally I was ready for my first night doing the nightly back-up. On March 5, 1985, it was snowing that evening and the temp was below freezing. I headed off to my first night of work and drove along a road where the speed limit reached 55 MPH. As I traveled on this stretch, a car approaching from the other direction started to merge into my lane. My first thought was — They'll straighten out. But, that did not happen. I slowed down, merging onto the right shoulder in effort to avoid them. The last thing I remembered was seeing their bright headlights full in front of me. We crashed head on.

As I came to, all I could see was broken glass everywhere and the hood of the car shoved up covering my view in front of me. I could hear a ticking sound and something dripping from the engine. Dan Hartman singing I Can Dream About You slowly came into awareness and was blearing from the speakers. I quickly changed radio stations before turning the stereo off in case Dad was next behind the wheel. A common practice with his intolerance for rock music. What was I thinking?! No one was ever driving THIS car again!!

The snow was falling on me making me wet. Cars were driving around us slowly and soon I heard sirens. Luckily, there was a firehouse just up the street. The driver's side of the car was totally caved in and the only way to get me out was through the passenger side. As the EMT's worked to maneuver and squeeze me out, I screamed my head off… clearly, this was the worst pain I had ever experienced. The ambulance took me to the closest trauma hospital.

There was definitely a sense of urgency around how I was being handled. As the gurney came through the ER doors, several doctors and nurses quickly descended on me. My clothes were cut and pulled off my body and I was prepared for x-ray. That process took a long time as I don't think there was a part of my body that didn't get filmed. The last thing to be x-rayed was my head. As the glass lens passed in front of me I could see my reflection. I thought, who poured red paint all over me? Not yet realizing that it was blood. Once all the x-rays were finished, they put me in a room and asked if I wanted them to call someone. I replied rather sheepishly, *"Can you please call my parents?"*

Mom was told over the phone that I had been in a car accident but, that I was stable. They both got in the car and drove to the hospital. Dad dropped Mom off at the emergency door and looked for parking. As Mom came into the room upon seeing me, she completely lost it! Frantically crying and screaming, touching me all over... The nurses had to tell her several times not to touch me as they were waiting for X-rays to be developed. She was so upset to see all the blood on me that she pulled out a balled up Kleenex from her purse, licked it and started to wipe my face. I actually had shards of glass imbedded in my forehead and her efforts to clean me up were adding to the pain. The nurses now had the additional task of getting her under control.

Considering both of my parent's reactions to seeing me, I must have looked a lot worse than they were expecting. When Dad entered the room, he turned white as a ghost. He pulled up a chair and sat at my head where I couldn't see him but, I could hear him. Listening to his voice, I tried to understand what he was saying to me. Then I realized, he was praying for me! Other than bedtime prayers when I was a kid, he had never done this before. His actions immediately reminded me of those early memories with him tucking me in at night and I felt comforted. His tone was shaky and emotional and for some reason, I wanted him there. Once again reminding me that he was, indeed the more capable parent. Much like when I was a little one...he would be patient and understanding with me when I suffered from chronic kidney infections. During the ages of four and five I would frequently have pain going to the bathroom. I remember seeing blood in the toilet which would yield a trip to the doctor to give a urine sample. Lots of time passed sitting on the toilet so afraid to go because I knew how bad it would hurt. If Mom took me in, she'd get frustrated and accuse me of exaggerating but, Dad would soften his voice and be patient even running the warm water in the sink and holding my hand in the stream to encourage me to let go. His other side could be so beautiful.

Laying on that hospital gurney in so much pain, I wanted to believe my parents could help carry this enormous experience and somehow make it better.

A couple of doctors finally entered the room with the results of all the x-rays. I had a dislocated right hip, a shattered right knee cap, and several broken ribs. My head had smashed through the windshield but thankfully there was no scull fracture. Mom's screams for painkillers were finally heard and they gave me morphine. I was astonished at how quickly the pain eased once they pushed the syringe into my IV. Next, I was wheeled down the hall to get ready to have my hip put back into it's socket. My shattered knee cap was put back together like puzzle pieces and I spent the next ten days in the hospital in traction with my knee immobilized.

They would not let me out of bed to walk until I was ready to go home. On day two, a team from plastic surgery came up to have a look. My head, face and hands had received more lacerations than could be counted. As they looked at my wounds they would remark how good I looked and that everything should heal up fine. I asked, *"Can I see myself in a mirror?"* They quickly pulled one out and handed it to me. Heal up fine?! I looked like a panther had attacked me. My knee was forced to stay straight for six weeks before physical therapy helped me to bend it again.

I spent the next several weeks in therapy pushing through a very painful recovery. I walked with crutches and followed orders from doctors to bring healing as quickly as possible. Everything hurt. Everything! *"Here, take these pills…"* Mom literally had a pharmacy in her bathroom medicine cabinet. She could never understand why I refused her pain pills. To take them would give opportunity to become like her and there was no way in hell I was allowing that.

Little did I know at the time how great this car accident would effect me in the years to come.

After a few months of mending and rehab I returned to my 2 separate 3M jobs. Everyone was happy to see I was alive and doing well. With my new lease on life I didn't want to waste anymore time. It was now time to have some fun. The weekends were all about going out with friends from my restaurant job. The ritual would start with a Saturday trip to the mall in search of a new outfit or maybe a new pair of shoes or boots…Even just a new belt sometimes would do to freshen up a look. Working two jobs while living at home with cheap rent did allow for a healthy shopping budget. I'd get all done up — spending a couple of hours getting the hair big and the makeup just right. The outfit had to be perfect and eye catching. Doused with whatever fragrance was popular at the time and then out to the bars we'd go.

There were so many great hot spots around town but, one of my favorite destinations was a bar on the east side of St. Paul where upstairs you could dance and rock-out listening to popular local bands cover artists like Van Halen, Mötley Crüe, Dokken, Scorpions and Def Leppard. Downstairs was a disco with a sunken, light up dance floor where DJs would play all this amazing dance music that I had never heard before. The Gap Band, Midnight Star, Dazz Band, The Time, Rick James! All new music to my ears. Big projector screens hung on the walls and everyone in the place would become perfectly still when the latest Michael Jackson video played. Upstairs, downstairs, back and forth all night long. It was such a great time to be young. Who might I meet tonight? Some new friends? Possibly a cute guy? There was no social media or cell phones. We met people organically, out in the wild! Typically at bar close, details would be shared about after parties to hit.

That 80's energy and spirit has never been duplicated. If only we could go back and visit it once in a while.

Of course I told Mom and Dad there was no alcohol and that we just wanted to dance. I'm pretty sure they didn't believe me.

Looking back I was attractive, but my girlfriends were beautiful. Guys would often approach me, start up a conversation and then ask me to introduce them to one of my friends. Of course these experiences did wonders at confirming the message I received so many years ago standing at the kitchen sink in my swimsuit. I'd watch my girlfriends meet guys, go out on dates and develop relationships. It was all quite amazing to me and and I couldn't begin to imagine doing the same.

A girlfriend of mine from high school was moving into an apartment with her older sister and they asked if I wanted to share the apartment and split the rent with them three ways. I was so desperate, I jumped at the chance to get out of my house. I eagerly agreed, packed up my things and moved in with them. They each had their own room but, I had to sleep out on the living room sofa. And, since it was party central in that place and I worked two jobs, I didn't last more than a couple of months. I then had an opportunity to move into a townhouse with three girls from the Ground Round where I would have my own room. After a few months, one of the girls moved out-of-state to go to college and another one joined the Navy so unfortunately, back home I went — to keep saving up for my great and final escape.

# Atlanta, GA

Dad came home from work one evening with an extra little kick in his step. He seemed different. Alive...more engaging. The devision of 3M he worked for was transferring to Atlanta, Georgia. They were offering to relocate him and he definitely wanted to go! No more frozen tundra and, much closer to his beloved South Carolina. His "contract" would be over and this move would make him a real employee with full benefits and a pension. I wasn't financially ready to move out on my own yet and warmer weather similar to my lovely California did seem attractive to me. Maybe I'll settle out there.

I drove down with Mom to look for housing. We found a suitable home in a suburb close to where Dad's new office would be. He soon followed and joined us. I immediately went out looking for work. Since I had experience working at a restaurant, I applied at a local Ruby Tuesdays. There were no hostess or waitress jobs available so, they put me to work in the kitchen as a prep cook. It was hard work and much different than what I was used to. One of our duties was to unload the food truck on delivery day. These chores certainly woke up my auto accident injuries and coming home on these days, I would struggle to get out of the car. They loved my work ethic and gave me plenty of hours.

Growing up in Southern California was a huge melting pot. I went to school and played with kids from multiple backgrounds. Black, white, hispanic, Asian, Indian, you name it! Our parents were all in similar economic situations and, our skin color was quite irrelevant. Minnesota was populated with lots of blond hair and blue eyes but, Atlanta brought back the diversity I was raised in and I liked that. What didn't come easy for me was making friends. I was a "Yankee" first of all, and by this age others were entrenched into the patterns of their routines, friends and families.

I missed my Minnesota girlfriends and the comfort of living where everything was familiar. I might have landed in the midwest some years ago kicking and screaming but, It has now become my home. Living in Atlanta, I missed Minnesota's sensibilities, it's warm, well-meaning people, and it's dependability.

Before leaving Minnesota for Atlanta, my parents had arranged for a Lawyer to handle my car accident. In the summer of 1986 my case settled out of court in my favor against the driver who hit me. My parents were hoping for much more but in the end, I was awarded $50,000. My Lawyer got a third of it and then I bought my parents a slightly used car. I felt obligated since their car was totaled in the accident. I didn't quite understand how everything worked back then nor did I realize how insurance had covered the loss. They certainly didn't protest and were happy to have the new car.

I immediately planned a trip to come back to the Twin Cities for a visit. As the plane circled for landing and I looked down at the landscape of the familiar lakes and trees, I felt my heart beating more soundly, recognizing I was truly back home. There was a lot of partying and MTV watching to pass the time but, one day I accompanied my friend I was staying with to the salon where she had an appointment to get her haircut. As I sat in the waiting area watching the stylists work, I got a brilliant idea!

I couldn't afford college and I didn't qualify for student loans because, apparently my Dad made too much money. He always said he wouldn't pay for my college because no one helped him. I knew the training was about a year and it was just glamorous enough to appeal to me. I would love to say that I chose to become a hairstylist because the profession called out to me and I knew it was the only thing I wanted to do but, that would be a lie. I chose it because of the affordable tuition and the timeline made sense and worked with the hand I was dealt.

Before I headed back to Atlanta, I visited a local Cosmetology school and put in a down payment for tuition. I also put down a security deposit on an apartment and shopped for a sectional sofa for my new living room. With the remainder of my settlement money, I finally had the funds to make the break. I will go to Cosmetology school for approximately ten months and if I'm careful, I will have just enough money to get me through until I could start working. A full-proof plan — and with it, I was ecstatic!

By now, Dad seemed to have given up on trying to control Mom. They rarely fought with each other anymore. Dad was ignoring Mom now the way he so often ignored me. Both of them separately were sneaking into my room and reading my journals — that I clearly didn't hide well enough. I would catch them asking me about things I had written about but had never discussed with them. I quit journaling. In fact, I left those journals behind and did not bring them with me. Let them read them! Let them know how much hell I was feeling all of those years. Maybe someday they'll understand why I had to leave.

I flew back to Georgia from my short trip to Minnesota and shared what I had done on my vacation. Securing an apartment, enrolling in school and even buying a sofa. Mom cried constantly trying again to make me feel responsible for her EVERYTHING! Dad told me that I would never make it. Being a Hairstylist was laughable to him. *"It's just a matter of time before you'll be back."* He said condescendingly.

Over my dead body! I put my notice in at my job and began making arrangements to have my bedroom furniture and some other belongings shipped out to Minnesota. Mom and Dad could not have been more unhappy about my plan but, I felt so secure in my decision to leave that it carried me through. I held no fear of the future... Only fear of what might be if I stayed. My survival instincts were working on overdrive, and I fully trusted my plan.

# No Place Like Home

It was exactly one week before Cosmetology school was starting. I had planned well and it was time to leave. My car was packed with things I would need right away in my new apartment. Dad left for work that morning giving me a very cordial goodbye like you would an acquaintance or someone you barely knew. Mom went on crying and following me around the house like a lost puppy. She was fixated on this notion that I would be raped and killed on my way to Minnesota. Meanwhile, I had my shield of protection around me and she was not able to affect me quite the way she was hoping. I held my own and told her everything was going to be fine and that it was time for me to go. I hugged her without shedding a tear and then turned my back to go out to the car. She stayed inside, waving at me through the kitchen window, crying the whole time as I drove away. Deep breath... I wonder if my tire marks are still visible on that driveway? The wheels of my car could not carry me away fast enough. Looking in the rearview mirror at the house as I drove away, I hoped not to see her coming out to chase me. The further I got away, the better I could breathe.

All the while on that long road trip, Control by Janet Jackson played on my cassette player. I must have listened through it at least fifty times before reaching Minnesota. The lead song very fitting to my circumstances. I car-danced my way north through those beautiful Tennessee mountains and beyond... I was finally free! My energy was high, and I could feel the hope building. It was such a stark contrast to the strangling heaviness living in my parent's home. I had carefully mapped out the trip, and on the first day made it all the way to Peoria, Illinois.

I was following a tight budget, so I found a very inexpensive motel off the main road to stay the night. The looks of it left a lot to be desired but, the price was right, and it was just one night. I turned the key and went into my room to find dark paneled walls, very worn, cheap green carpeting, an old crappy bed, and a nonworking TV. I called the front desk to see if something could be done about the TV. All I wanted to do was lie in bed, veg-out watching a little television and go to sleep. Shortly thereafter, I get a knock at my door. I open it to a grubby middle-aged handyman with a cart full of tools. As he tinkered with the TV, he flirted with me uncomfortably, trying to convince me to come have a little fun at the bar next-door. I shrugged it off, saying how tired I was from the long drive, and probably wouldn't go. He went on trying to convince me otherwise all the while, interjecting poorly stated compliments and looking hard at me — giving me major creeps. Finally, he got the TV working and reluctantly left the room. Just as the door closed, I saw the keychain on his belt looking like he had every room key on him. A queasy feeling settled into my stomach and I couldn't help but think about Mom's crazy prediction. I bolted and chain locked the door. Even shoved a chair up underneath the door knob to be extra safe. Nothing and no one was going to screw with my plan! Who knew venturing out on your own would be so scary — so exhausting? Soon I fell asleep and didn't wake until morning.

The next day, I hit the road early and made it the rest of the way to Minnesota by early afternoon. That first night I slept on the floor at my new apartment, with my new sectional sofa due to arrive the next day. My bed, clothes, and other items would be arriving a few days later. I spent the rest of that week nesting and getting my apartment just right, complete with a giant blowup Godzilla in the living room looking out the patio window and a life-size poster of Jon Bon Jovi hanging in the entryway. I was ready to start my new life. September 8, 1986 was the first day of Cosmetology school. I drove to downtown Saint Paul, parked and walked the couple of blocks to the corner of 6th street and St Peter. Here, my new Cosmetology school filled two floors of the historic corner store front. As I walked through the doors and looked around the place, I had not a clue in regards to what was in front of me. And yet, I had no fear. I could not have been more certain I was exactly where I was supposed to be.

There were approximately 20 people in my class. We had 6 weeks of basic training strictly in classroom, working on mannequin heads. Then, we advanced to the clinic floor to actually practice doing hair on real people. Everyone seemed eager to dig in and also equally quite clueless. There was a shy, quiet girl named Christy in my class who I started up a conversation with and discovered that we lived very close to each other. It turned out, she was the younger sister of a girl I graduated from high school with. Oh yeah, I see the resemblance. We decided to start carpooling to save money on parking. She looked like a Christy! Blonde hair, blue eyes, very pretty and sweet. The girl next door... We clicked right away and became fast friends. Not long after, we made the acquaintance of two other girls who were already friends that started in the class right after us. Chantal had dark wavy hair and very large brown exotic eyes. She seemed to have plenty of street smarts coupled with a very soft tender heart. Kathie definitely had the leadership gene. She recently left college to go to Cosmetology school instead — and she was a single Mom of an adorable seven-month-old baby boy, who we all adored! The four of us became inseparable and we hung out with each other constantly. We went out almost every night! Hitting the bars that had weekly specials like "quarter beers" and "dollar drinks." Kathie was a pro at finding all the deals and we took full advantage!

We called ourselves "The Party Dolls" and even had sweatshirts made up with our names on them. Maybe the first ever Cosmetology school sorority. All the crazy shenanigans we were a party to... the thought of them brings an immediate smile and chuckle every time! Those great girls provided for me a much needed opportunity to cut loose and blow off some steam. And I SO BADLY needed to blow off some steam!

"The Party Dolls"

# Lee Anne

1,550 hours, that's how long it takes in the state of Minnesota to complete Cosmetology school. In order to get your license to practice, you have to pass a lengthy written test and an almost all-day practical test as well. Thankfully, I passed both of my tests on the first try and soon I had my license in hand. My lawsuit money was all gone now and I had started waitressing the last couple of months before graduating to help pay the bills. The plan was to find a job doing hair in the Salon five days a week and work the other two days and some evenings waitressing. That plan unfortunately provided less opportunity for Party Doll shenanigans. I applied at several salons, interviewed at a couple and landed at a Regis salon in downtown St. Paul just a couple of blocks from where I had gone to school. My nerves were mixed with excitement arriving for my first day of work. My shift started at 9am that day. All the other girls starting with me that morning seemed quite indifferent about me being there. Some were actually downright rude. I guess everyone was struggling to make a living, and with the addition of me on the floor, this apparently took money from their paychecks. I heard them talking with each other asking... *"Why on earth would our manager hire another stylist?"*

As the next shift started, a very tall, thin girl with long dark curly hair came up to me and started talking. She was built like a runway model, fresh off the catwalk... Beautiful. Her make up was perfect and there was not a hair out of place. *"Oh hi! You must be new... What's your name? My name is Lee Anne. Actually, my first name is Lee and my middle name is Anne but everybody calls me Lee Anne. Is this your first salon? I worked at 'Erica's Elegance' for like five months before here but I didn't like it. She was a powerhead! I'm kind of new here too... Where did you go to Cosmetology school? Oh, my younger sister went there!... Oh hey, my older sister is meeting me for lunch today. Do you want to come with us?"*

I honestly don't think she took a breath between sentences. I would start to answer her questions, and she would immediately start talking again. I thought, who is this wacky chick?! But, I just went with it. Someone at my new salon was being nice to me, and I was very happy about that! I went to lunch with her and her sister that first day. We worked a lot of the same hours and although wacky she was, there was something very genuine and lovely about her that made me feel energized and yet safe in her presence. She was unlike anyone I had ever met. I was always so lucky to have such good friends in my life and they were all so good to me...their families too. I was often invited over for dinners and holidays.

Lee Anne had a large extended family and they were all very connected with each other. Her Mom, her two sisters, grandparents, several aunts and uncles, and oodles of cousins would gather together anytime there was a birthday to celebrate. They did outdoor picnics together for Memorial Day and the Fourth of July. Of course, they would all come together for the big holidays too... everyone bringing lots of food! They knew each other so well and celebrated each other's talents and accomplishments. I would hear them ask one another questions, and then follow up questions based on responses they received. And then, they would listen — really listen with care, concern or, excitement. They'd kid around, giving each other grief in a playful way and yet, would stand up and back each other — because they were family. There was an acceptance and comfortableness they shared with one another that I had not known in my family. Witnessing them love each other the way they did was so beautiful to me. And, I loved being in the midst of this atmosphere.

Lee Anne was a single mother to a two-year-old, little girl. She named her Terra, because she said she grounded her. What an incredible mother, balancing the right amount of discipline when necessary with an enormouse expression of love, that was given so genuinely — so freely. I remember thinking, is this how a mother is supposed to love her daughter? Growing up in a rougher part of town gave her an "edge." When pushed, there was a feistiness in her that naturally came out. I used to tease her about her toughness.

*"You can take the girl off of Rice Street, but you can't take the Rice street out of the girl."* Lee Anne was a take the bull by the horns kind of girl — not afraid of anyone. It would amaze me how she handled difficulty. So different we were, but something in me pulled close to her, and I haven't stepped away since. She and I began a friendship that first day we worked together.

To date, I think we are going on thirty-seven years. We have had our disagreements from time to time...we always get through them. Our friendship has taught me that with time, you can actually trust others. And I have come to trust Lee Anne fully.

**Lee Anne and I over the years**

# Fake It Till You Make It

My Salon work schedule was Tuesday through Saturday and then I would waitress on Sunday and Monday. Cosmetology school teaches the basics and having a license made me legit. But now, working in the Salon is where the true training begins. I had a lot to learn — not just how to execute excellent hair but, also how to be professional and confident with people. I didn't have time to be scared. Paying for rent and eating regularly took top focus. It takes years to become established in this profession. Exposure to enough clients to encourage return visits adequate to fill your schedule, that transpires to a paycheck to live off of doesn't happen quickly — or without a lot of hard work and long hours.

Once a month I was required to work a Saturday graveyard shift at the restaurant. I'd drive home in the wee hours of Sunday morning thinking I was seeing things jump out on the road in front of me. Those early years were exhausting and seemed to take a toll with me getting sick with random colds and flu more often.

It must have been the "high" of being out on my own that energized me to keep up because I got through it all without a complaining spirit.

Once my year lease was up on my apartment, I moved in with a friend of a friend from my old Ground Round job to split the rent. That move eventually allowed me to quit waitressing. Lee Anne and I left Regis together and embarked into the suburbs where the clientele was more stay-at-home Moms getting haircuts, colors, highlights, and perms. They'd bring in their kids for haircuts, with the Dad's filling up our evenings and Saturdays. Being in a large strip mall with free parking was nice too. We received regular on-going training and my skills behind the chair increased greatly during this time. We had a staff of all young women our age. A fellow stylist Corrine, was one I so looked up to. She was so precise with her hair cutting. I would watch and learn. She possessed poise and professionalism that I lacked, yet so badly needed. I wonder if she knows how much she helped me.

The long distance calls to and from Georgia were so difficult. Dad never got on the phone — only when he'd answer accidentally to which he'd immediately hand the phone over to Mom. She would go on for quite some time crying and telling me how awful it was without me there, or she'd unleash her ugliness and insults letting me know how disappointing I was to have left her. Up until this point in my life, when Mom said jump, I jumped as high as I could. Moving out was really my first act of defiance against her. Our phone calls were never an opportunity for me to gain support. I had to gather that elsewhere. My brother, his wife and I would fly out for Christmas. He was so lucky! Since he was married, they alternated Christmases with his wife's family. I had no choice but to go every year. Those times by myself were especially difficult. Dad would go out of his way to find fault. He held zero respect for my chosen profession and assumed I was living a life of debauchery. Mom would persist in begging me to come back. One Christmas while we were all there, Dad asked if we wanted to drive over and see his office. My brother, his wife and I jumped in the car for something to do that would be a welcomed distraction. The office was closed due to the holidays but, once we arrived, one of Dad's co-workers was there catching up on some work. He introduced my brother and his wife — and then me. His colleague looked surprised when shaking my hand. *"Norman, I didn't know you had a daughter!"* That moment conveyed many messages to me that didn't help Dad's and my relationship any. He seemed to have heard about my brother — even his wife. But, it was very apparent that his hairstylist daughter was not talked about at the water cooler.

My brother jokingly referred to those trips at Christmas as "The Sleigh Ride To Hell." Once back home in Minnesota, my friends would often remark how different I was. Troubled...withdrawn. Usually it would take me a few weeks to detox. I would cope by going out and drinking heavily night after night. Luckily, I was a happy drunk and that was a better place to be. This kind of drinking was different from the party drinking I did with my friends. I was so eager to undo and forget…needing desperately to erase Dad's disgusted looks and comments. Quite Mom's tantrums and insults. Put aside the reality that neither of them knew me at all. And, I so badly wanted to be known and wanted. Thankfully, after a couple of weeks or so, I would pivot and tire of the practice of drinking and return to healthier ways. Looking back, things could have gone very differently for me without that pivot.

A few years after I left Georgia, Mom and Dad seemed to be settling into a more peaceful existence with each other. They were fighting less and actually spending more time together. By now Mom was using oxygen more and more and one day after they had returned home from a drive, their car had overheated and the oxygen tanks stored in the garage started to blow up. It was a horrendous fire. They were able to get out of the house safely, but the house was a total loss. The calls back-and-forth were constant. Mom, traumatized so badly would beg for me to come and save her again. The house was fully insured and they were able to rebuild an even nicer house once it was all said and done. In hindsight and even now, I regretted leaving my journals behind… All of that outpouring burned to dust. I'm saddened that I'll never read them again.

# I'm Sorry

Mom was sick as far back as my memories live. Either truly sick from her medical accident and what that left behind or, sick from what the drugs were doing to her. Now, due to her esophagus and lung injuries along with decades of chronic smoking, the oxygen tanks were replaced by a permanent unit that provided tubing to access the entire house. Her health continued to decline and less than a decade after having to rely on oxygen, she was literally bedridden. Walking to the bathroom and back would leave her completely out of breath. In March of 1994, Dad suggested that my brother and I come see her as her condition had worsened in the three months since Christmas. I flew in to find her breathing so labored that she was now doing frequent nebulizer treatments. During that trip, I slept out on the living room sofa so I could get up in the night to help her with her treatments. Dad was still working full-time and it gave him a break to get a full nights sleep.

I woke one night to hear her calling my name to come help her. I went to her side to administer her breathing treatment and as she started to feel a little relief and breath a bit easier, she laid there staring at me sadly. I felt another guilt session was coming but, with teary eyes she pulled the breathing mask away from her face she simply said, *"I'm sorry."* I took it as an apology for getting me up in the middle of the night to help her. I assured her I didn't mind and that it was no problem at all…to which she grabbed my arm while shaking her head and said again, *"I'm sorry."* The way she was looking at me, I knew exactly what she was referring to. She was apologizing for all of it. For the possessive treatment. For the conditional love. For the drugs. For running away with me leaving me no choice but to go with her. For neglecting me. For the hateful horrible way she would talk to me. For taking out all her frustration and putting it on me. For bruising my body and doing worse to my heart. For making me responsible for her well being and happiness. For chasing me away, and making it so hard to come visit. She was apologizing for all of it. Growing up, I listened to so many apologies from her that they sincerely grew to mean nothing. This time was somehow different and in that moment, I felt the weight of her apology. And I forgave her. Ever since, I have forgiven her more times than I can count. Again…and again…

At the end of that week I flew back home to Minnesota, and two weeks later on March 31, 1994 in the wee hours of that Thursday morning before daylight, I was awakened by the phone ringing. *"Hello?"* It was Dad… *"Barbara, your mother passed away last night in her sleep. She's gone."*

I was 29 when Mom died. I did not realize how young that actually was back then. As much as this news should not have surprised me, with Mom rallying and recovering more times than I could have possibly counted, I was in total shock. Three hours later I was on a plane back to Georgia. I worked really hard to keep it together on that flight but, was not very successful. Sitting in that window seat looking out, I was able to keep the crying convulsions at a minimum but, the tears streamed down my cheeks without stopping.

I was pressed in between two very hard places. Part of me was completely devastated. Mom had such a huge presence in my life. How was I to go on without that? I also felt a huge weight was lifted and a sense of relief knowing the difficulty of our relationship would now be over. I had failed in her expectations of me to be her all… Everything she lived for. I turned my back on her, moving away and leaving her all alone to sit in despair. The guilt was suffocating. Guilt for not saving her and, guilt for feeling freed from the impossible task.

Over the week, Dad, my brother and I arranged for Mom's funeral. Candy Grandma and my three aunts flew in, we met with the funeral director, made choices, did all the things…Looking back at photos of that week, I look so fragile. The things I needed most were not present. Reassurance, the comfort of being held, someone to understand the complexity of the relationship ending and an ear to hear. None of that was present for me. I continued doing what I knew…disregarding my needs and putting on a persona of strength that was not at all real.

Once back home in Minnesota, sleeping through the night was almost impossible. I swear, I'd feel Mom's body weight laying on top of me. Smothering me. Once I even shouted aloud, *"Mom! Get off of me!!!"* To which I then felt the weight lift. The grieving continued throughout the next months. Mother's Day was approaching and to distract myself, I went out and bought flowers and then planted them in pots and flower boxes surrounding the deck. That night Mom visited me in my sleep again. This time there was no smothering. Instead, she was vibrant and healthy! There was a smile on her face and she was warm and engaging. I almost didn't recognize this version of her but, remembered seeing it in old photos…long before I had come along. She told me that she saw the flowers I planted and thought that they were so beautiful.

I have never quite been able to fully process all the facets of our relationship. All these years later, when her memory comes to mind, I try to focus on those times when she tried. The white go-go boots, coming to see me in my school plays, waking me up in the middle of the night to watch the royal wedding of Charles and Dianna because she thought I'd love it!

But, if I am totally honest with myself, I grieve what was meant to be but, never was. And then I choose to forgive her…again.

I now wondered if Dad and I would have a chance at a real relationship. I was no longer a needed pawn to passive aggressively lash out through. Mom died the last day of March and Dad was remarried by the end of October. I have to give him credit…he went big and tracked down a woman he graduated high school with that he always had a big crush on. She was now divorced and available. A few letters from Dad did the trick to turn her head and he was as giddy as a school boy. I first found out about her existence when he announced they were getting married.

Imagine being in deep water without the ability to swim. With arms flailing and legs kicking, you balance back-and-forth between gasping for air and drowning. Although a terrible strategy, it was how I managed to survive so far. And I was so exhausted. As I grieved Mom's death, my high school fantasies of exiting this world had come back and were comforting me like an old friend. Relationships were so difficult for me. I would always overprotect — sabotaging closeness. At times, I would entertain these crazy dreams of finding someone, getting married and becoming a mother. But, deep in my innermost knowing, I knew that would never be my future. Realistically, I couldn't imagine even getting close. Self-loathing was as much a part of me as my brown eyes and freckles. It went everywhere with me like a pesky kid sister I would fight with, and then protect. I agreed with it, which made it that much more unlikely to leave. The only hope I could see of being freed from it was through my own end.

I tried to share my turmoil with close friends but, the subject was far too heavy, and they were not able to carry it. For the first time in my life, I broke down and sought therapy. I was put on antidepressant medication which numbed my emotions and I went to weekly therapy sessions for a few months. I wish I could say it helped. It didn't, so I quit.

Suicide was no longer an "if," but a "when" and the time was drawing near.

# Who Said That?

It is now the summer of 1994 and I have just turned thirty. Lee Anne got married a couple of years prior and was expecting her second baby. Christy was married in the last year and was also pregnant. Their due dates were less than two weeks apart. I had been a bridesmaid in both of their weddings, and now they were both becoming Moms! I honestly could not have been more excited for these two. I felt happiness for them, and excitement at the knowledge of relief for myself coming on the horizon. I made a plan that after they both had given birth, I would finally end my pain. The plan was to wait for my roommate to leave for work, and then I would go down into the garage and start my car with a full tank of gas, leaving the garage door closed.

I needed to wait because I couldn't bear the thought of my actions upsetting either of these dear friends to the point it affected their pregnancies. Lee Anne went first. Two days later, Christy had a son. As Lee Anne entered into labor, I waited with her family for the new arrival. I was certain it was a boy, but we would all be surprised to find out together. Her labor went on for hours. They were using medication to induce her, but things were moving very slowly. It was sometime around 10 PM that the nurses convinced us to go home because she was only dilated to a four and this process was likely to go on for several hours. With my purse over my shoulder, I was saying goodbye to her sisters when suddenly the nurse popped back out of the room and yelled down the hall to us. *"She's dilated to a ten! The baby is coming!"* Well, that was fast!? We are not going home now!

I slid my purse back off of my shoulder and we anxiously waited. I was right! A boy it was, and I couldn't wait to meet him. My level of depression was so deep, but somehow I was over the moon with this blessing! Lee Anne's mother was in the room with her and her husband, while I waited outside in the hallway with her daughter and her sisters… We were so excited, and it was all we could do to not barge straight through that door. Once the doctors and nurses left the room, they were cleaned up and finally ready for company. Lee Anne's husband asked me if I wanted to hold him. He and I had been "team boy" all along. I wanted to hold that baby more than anything in the world. Reaching out with such eagerness, he was put into my arms. My focus was so strong that everyone and everything in the room practically disappeared. His sheer beauty took my breath away. His little hands and fingers were so tiny and perfect. His face was so soft and sweet. The tiniest perfect, dark eyelashes. His black full head of hair! As I held him, taking inventory of all his little charms, beauty, and potential, something very odd happened.

As loud and clear as anything on this earth I heard,

*"This is what I see when I look at you."*

It landed on me like a waterfall — Like warm soft air coming from the back of my head and flowing over top of me past my shoulders, chest, lap and down my legs. I was so startled! Who said that? Was I the only one who heard it? I later went home and kept thinking about what I heard. Was it all in my own mind? Wishful thinking? Or, was God speaking straight to me? I didn't know. But from that moment on, I was changed. Something huge shifted and I didn't consider suicide an option ever again. A day later, his parents gave him the name Chase. God certainly used him to chase me down. A beautiful bond was appointed, and a true relationship started. I felt the warmth of this blessing like the bright sun hitting my face on a cold day. Hope… It was sheer hope. An expectation of the unknown.

Mondays were my "Chase days." I'd get all my stuff done and head over to Lee Anne's in the late morning. He'd usually be waking from his morning nap and now it was playtime, then followed by lunchtime. Feeding him was a mess with spoon airplanes coming in for a landing, followed by bath time. Lots of splashing with floaty toys and then time to dry him off and get him dressed. We would play until he couldn't keep his little eyes open any longer.

I'd hang around during his afternoon nap and after, we would take him for a walk in his stroller or, out on shopping excursions. When school let out, Lee Anne's daughter sometimes had an after school event to go to. Girl's fast pitch softball or a track meet. I'd be there for it all...convincing myself that I was there to help but, I was definitely the winner here. As Chase grew into a toddler, I'd sometimes take him with me and run all my day-off errands. Strangers would tell me how adorable my son was. I loved that people thought he was mine! Pretending that this child was my own raised me to a higher level, and I so loved being there! As he grew, our bond strengthened, and I was often shocked at his reaction when I would arrive or leave. He lit up like a Christmas tree when I came over. No one had ever made me feel that way. To be wanted on such a pure and genuine level. It was shocking to me how this experience felt, and I realized, it's because I had never felt it before. I quite didn't know how to take it. I was thirty years old and still completely blinded to my worth.

One day when I was headed to their house, Lee Anne told little Chase I was coming over — later. But at his tender toddler age, he didn't understand the concept of "later." Their house had a full length, sidelight window next to their front door. As I walked up their walkway, I saw him laying in a heap on the floor asleep with his enormous stuffed animal and blanket. I knocked on the window and his head popped up! The expression on his face, I had never seen before on anyone. Little Chase still had tears in his eyes but his exuberance to get the door open took charge. Later, Lee Anne told me she regretted telling him so soon that I was on my way over. Apparently there were lots of tears, and he would not leave the front door until I got there. Some would call this occurrence cute or sweet but for me, it was hugely significant in helping me to see reality. I literally couldn't see what was true. But, this little boy made my heart sing. And I couldn't seem to get enough.

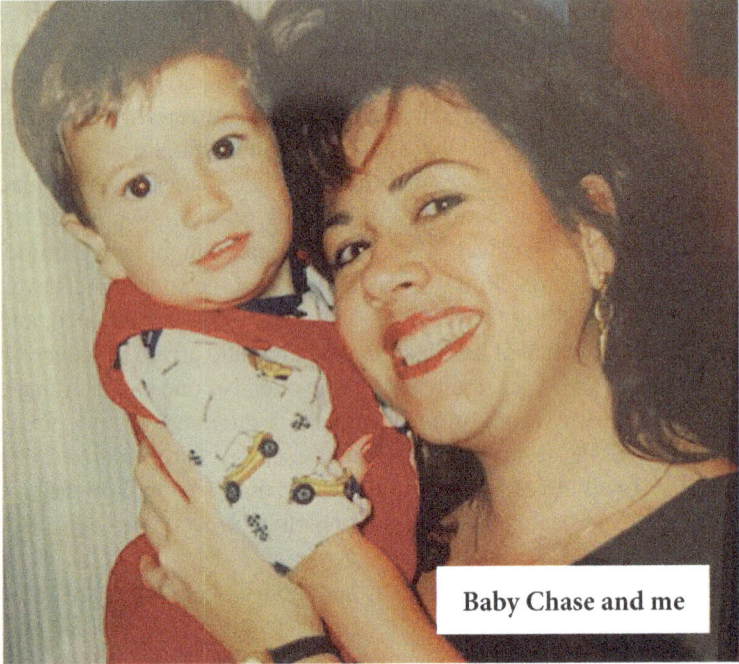

**Baby Chase and me**

As Chase grew from toddler to pre-school age, his parents enrolled him in a nursery school just up the street from their house. It happened to be part of a Lutheran church and school that was well respected in the community but, I'm pretty sure it was chosen because of its close location. The daily practice of prayer and other things that were being taught were making their way home. Lee Anne would share with me, when Chase got hurt he would ask her to pray for him, and with his sweet innocence he would tell her, *"Jesus lives in our hearts, Mommy."* We found that we were both moved by this and it started me thinking about those early years in my little Baptist church in Orange County where I had learned that too, but then somehow forgot.

Around this same time, the salon I worked at employed this young exuberant part-time receptionist. I wanted for myself the outlook that she carried. Her joy and kindness spoke beautifully and even though she was just over a decade younger than me, I learned from her. She was a college student at a nearby Christian school and she would often talk about one of her professors and how he taught the Bible. Her description of him intrigued me and I wanted to know more. This professor had recently started pastoring a new church that by chance, was meeting weekly at a high school just a few blocks from where I lived at the time. It was gaining quite the reputation and I couldn't help but notice the huge traffic jam every Sunday as church let out. Clients of mine and others were talking positively about it too so, I decided to show up one Sunday. And then the next, and the next.

The atmosphere was quite different than the usual church environment with an alter, pews or stained glass windows. We met in a large auditorium where the high quality music was more rock and R&B — which I loved. Those cords would hit some unrecognized spot within and the tears would fall. I would see other people tear up and often lift their hands during worship. I wasn't quite sure what I thought about that. I'd see people taking down notes and others singing with enthusiasm and beaming like my salon receptionist. It was all a little odd for me, but the emotion on people's faces was genuine and I couldn't deny that.

The pastor was young and full of energy and passion. His brown curly hair and slightly hyper delivery made him hard to miss. He talked about God in the most unique ways. Preaching urgently about this enormous love pursuing and chasing us down to pour out over us. To heal what hurts. To fix what's broken…setting us on a path to the life we were meant for. As he would deliver these messages, his sheer certainty was so compelling that I couldn't seem get enough. Week after week this message was getting through to me and I found myself gaining more hope. Hope that was first ignited when I held little Chase late on the night he was born. Now, I was feeling it activating in my muscles…quickening my steps and lifting the heaviness that had made it's home in my heart.

I spent the next eleven years involved in that church. Taking every class I could, learning practical spiritual skills to apply to my life. Excited for what was to come every Sunday service. I became a regular fixture there and volunteered where I could. I learned from some really great seasoned people who did an awesome job of modeling this love.

That church experience has traveled along with me ever since. It was there that I realized, no matter how alone I am, that when I look to my left or to my right and see no one, I am never alone. This God who pursues me, chases me down and whispers in my ear when I am holding His beautiful creation, a message of love and acceptance... always with me — healing what hurts. Fixing what's broken.

# Not Me

Entering into a spiritual journey was a huge reset for me. The need to kick and flail to avoid drowning was becoming less necessary. I was now learning how to tread water, allowing my lungs to breath with consistency and finding ways to keep the waters more peaceful. For a good year or more I literally felt like God had me tucked in extra close. I felt His watch over me and noticed His careful attention as if I had my own personal tutor.

By now, several life preservers have been tossed my way and over the years I have learned how to fully utilize them. I found myself drawn to welcoming, energized people who I could learn a great deal from as I traveled through my 30s. Through many of the classes I attended at church, a spotlight shown on the abundance of limiting beliefs I carried about myself. I won't become a wife, or a mother. What will I become? I haven't a clue. Where do I begin to emerge out of these beliefs? So, I put my head down and dug in…relying on my work ethic because that's what I knew. By the age of 33, I was able to quit renting apartments with roommates, and actually bought a small townhome. It was nothing special and in a questionable part of town but, I fixed it up and three years later in a better market, it sold for almost double what I paid for it. Then, I really surprised myself by buying a house! A real Home! A small character rich 1940s bungalow, with hardwood floors throughout and a fireplace in the living room. It nestled in a lovely old neighborhood about 4 miles from downtown Minneapolis. The homes in the area were built between the early to mid 1900s, and although they were all close to each other, they were very different with European influences, making each one stand out. Looking all the way down the street was like looking at a beautiful jeweled necklace. The streets were lined with tall mature trees providing shaded walks throughout the neighborhood. Homes in this area were well cared for with creative, beautiful gardens gracing front yards. I remember the first time I came to look at my house. Walking up the steps into the front yard, my honest-to-God thoughts were, this is the kind of house other people get to live in, not me. I was certain something would prevent it from becoming mine but, I couldn't have been more wrong. I was approved and soon after, closed on my new home.

Never before have I enjoyed living in a dwelling as much as I did in my Orange County home with the vaulted ceilings and custom painted rooms until I moved into this house. I was now in a place that I felt perfectly content in. The size was just perfect for me and my dog Harley. A couple of years prior, Lee Anne's Mom needed to re-home her four month old collie/border collie mix puppy. She was then in her early sixties and still working as a full-time nurse with this pup way too much for her to handle. I remember the day well as she was discussing what to do with him. The words, *"I'll take him!"* came out of my mouth before I could even think. What have I just done? I had grown up having dogs but, was brokenhearted each time we moved as Dad had dealt with our dogs by driving them out into the country and just dumping them. I have cried my eyes out numerous times and still do over those memories. My brother once told me that as they drove off, our dogs chased the car for a long time before he couldn't see them anymore when he was encouraged to accompany Dad on one particular dumping. Each time, it was thoroughly traumatizing for me, and I have never spoken about it. Dad was certain that someone would find them and take them home, and I prayed hard he was right.

I brought that four month old puppy home to my place and a new relationship was born that gave me gifts I never thought were possible. He taught me unconditional love everyday of his life. At first this pup was quite the handful. Up early with an abundance of energy every morning meant, no more sleeping in! Obedience training and long walks helped him to fall into line. We would walk our neighborhood daily, and I was so proud to call it all home. I made acquaintances with my neighbors and they all knew my dog's name. Harley was all the company I needed and we were connected in a way I wouldn't have believed possible if I hadn't lived it.

A couple of months after moving into my new home, I received a call one night from my aunt telling me that Candy Grandma was quickly failing. She was having mini strokes and they were coming with more frequentcy. I had been back to visit a couple of times over recent years and witnessed her health deteriorating. On my last visit with her, she had become bedridden. Sitting in her room watching her beloved Law and Order, we'd chat during the commercials. She complained about her condition and how it took so much from her. Grass didn't grow readily under her feet…always with a task at hand and put together from head to toe, being stuck in bed did not match Grandma's personality at all! She still kept her hair colored, a perfect 7N in Hairstylist's language. I asked her, *"Grandma, if you had to choose one over the other, what would be better, having command of your body or your mind?"* She thought about it for a minute and answered *"Well, if I didn't have my mind we wouldn't be able to talk with each other like we are right now."*

My aunt's call came as I was financially tapped out from my move but, I needed to go see her. I put airfare on my credit card and flew in right away. They told her that I was coming and she waited for me. As I arrived and made it through the house full of relatives to her room, I was told that she could no longer talk. But, I'll never forget in a million years the look in her eyes when she saw me. She looked at me with such a sense of love and understanding, almost as if she knew things I didn't. I believe that she could see in my eyes how much she always meant to me, and still did. *"I love you, Grandma!"* She mouthed back to me slowly in silence, *"I love you too."*

By the end of the day, her eyes closed and never opened again. I hope she knew what a rescuer she was.

Candy Grandma and me

At this point, I was the last "Party Doll" still doing hair. Most all of my girlfriends were married by now and creating families.

My feeble attempts at dating were consistently dreadful. Those who were interested in me were never at all what I was looking for and, vice versa. I am no longer hanging out regularly at bars where meeting guys was the routine. Off and on I tried my hand at on-line dating but, that proved to be thoroughly disappointing as well. Friends and acquaintances would occasionally set me up on blind dates but, they were always complete fiascos. There were a ton of first time dates and a few short-term relationships that eventually ended. My self-loathing and inability at self-assuredness made it all so difficult for me to imagine myself worthy of someone's love and affection. As much as I wanted it, I was completely certain that it would never be mine.

Let's see… I remember after one particular date I was told that there wouldn't be a second because, I just *"wasn't what he was looking for."* I was told more times than I could count that I'd be prettier if I lost weight. One guy I was set up with who had recently been dumped sat in a both across from me crying the whole evening. I remember looking up at the clock on the wall thinking... If I leave right now, I can still catch Saturday Night Live. But, the nail in the coffin was from a guy who actually asked me if he could bring a girl to a party I invited him to. I had a huge crush on him and that slap in the face paralyzed me for a very long time.

All of it did a great job of confirming Dad's perceived message all those years ago standing at my kitchen sink. I can feel the wet swim suit on my skin, the glass of water in my hand, and the weight of my beach towel hanging around my neck. My life experience has me out the door immediately when there is the slightest hint of rejection. I don't deal with it gracefully but instead, pick up on the act of disinterest as further more abandonment. My need to protect myself outweighs everything ...every time.

Who could possibly find me desirable? Who could be deep and sensitive enough to see through me and push past my roadblocks to care for my fragile heart? Who had the patience to wait long enough to allow me to feel safe in his presence, encouraging me to recognize my best and allow it to emerge? That man never appeared. Instead, I found the complete opposite. I continued to keep my eyes open at church, hoping to find someone who would share my new found values but, as the years drifted by, somewhere along the way that dream drifted away as well.

I'm sure they don't mean to but, the way married people or those with life partners make single people feel is quite horrifying. Lucky for so many, they find a suitable match and feel quite certain of the other's interest in them that the relationship grows very organically. The question mark that their face carries when meeting me and learning that I am not married nor never have been is quite pronounced. *"What's wrong with you?"* Is a question I have been asked more than once. Maybe phrased a bit differently but nonetheless, letting me know they think it's a conscious decision I have made and they don't get it. I have received much judgement from others in regards to my single life and I'd be lying if I said it didn't hurt. But, I'm happy for them that they don't understand… I hope for no one to carry this level of disgust and self hate.

At some point along my life's journey I adopted the practice of ascribing love to food. I'm unaware of when it really started… possibly during puberty where my first bouts of depression began cycling. Food, or especially certain types of food equaled love, comfort, peace. There were seasons where I needed less of this love and then again, seasons where I needed it more. This reflected in my constant weight fluctuations that were noticed by everyone around me. When the weight was under control, compliments were abound! *"You look amazing!" "You're getting skinny!"* All delivered with the most upbeat enthusiasm.

When the pounds showed, the looks from others would travel up and down my body and I would want to run and hide. Hiding of course, would offer the opportunity for more food "love sessions." I have ridden this weight roller coaster my entire adult life. My lifelong self loathing affected other's view of me and I took their rejection so personally… This rejection pushed me deeper into seclusion where I had to retreat to feel safe and quiet honestly, remaining single was the best way to protect myself.

# Treading Water

Those who were around me were not aware of what tormented me. I have learned to perform for others my whole life, and now as an adult, I performed to look normal, well-adjusted and happy. My friends actually believed I had my act together better than most — because that's certainly how things appeared. My faith was now my raft to climb onto, and it held me up giving me tools and applications that worked to interrupt the direction I had drifted so far. This growth was slow and quite painful at times but, God took his time to never rush me.

As time passed, I thankfully continued to grow in my career. All those years ago I might have chosen my profession out of necessity but now, It's pushing me forward and I have come to honestly love it. Creating shapes through cutting hair and helping individuals feel good about themselves was good work for me to put my hands to. I continued to grow in my abilities, consistently working at being better behind the chair. I had the rapport and people pleasing down to a science and as the years passed, I became better and better at yielded a loyal returning clientele. I have always invested in ongoing training to stay relevant in a constantly changing field. Work ethic has been a natural gift I have been blessed with, and being a successful full-time hairstylist requires you to go hard after business and opportunity in order to write your paycheck. It's actually a very hard job that most people don't have a clue as to all that it encompasses. I am proud of the work life I have created for myself. And, with the unconditional love my dog provided along with my spiritual journey, I experienced a slow paced healing that grew internally little by little.

Dad and I spoke occasionally on the phone…all surface conversation. *"What's your weather like?"* — *"How's work?"*— *"Is your car running ok?"* Once he gathered my answers, the obligatory call was over. He never shared his life with me. My questions would yield very short answers and a hurriedness to get off the phone.

A decade earlier after Mom's death, I had waited as long as I could to meet his new wife. My reluctance had nothing to do with her at all...it was just too soon for me. About a year had passed since Mom was gone and our first meeting was when I flew down for Dad's surgery. Six months into their marriage, he was diagnosed with prostate cancer. Hardly being sick a day in his life, Dad did not want to admit he was scared. But I could hear the fear in his voice. My brother picked me up at the airport and drove me to the house. It was my first time back since Mom had died. As we walked in from the garage, my Dad's wife June stood there in the kitchen all smiles wearing one of my Mom's aprons that she had made. I noticed her natural brown hair had very little grey considering her age. A stark contrast to my Mom's pure white hair since she was in her early 50's. Her southern accent was turned up high! Something I knew my Dad loved. He finally had his sweet southern bell. As I stared at the apron remembering it, she must have sensed what I was thinking because she quickly took it off and hung it on the pantry door. She was a lovely, kind hearted person. Everything my mother was not, and Dad adored her!

He got through the surgery and on his way to a full recovery. I still struggled to be in his presence and only managed one or two more visits before I decided I was done spending my money and time visiting where I came back home to Minnesota losing ground and furthermore damaged.

I knew my Dad could show love. I witnessed it firsthand as I've seen him offer it to others multiple times. Our photo together in that man's garage so many years ago proved it! Those rare occasions when he would turn his attention in my direction... I swear, I could see his heart open. In those moments when he smiled, his eyes welcomed. My response would cause warmth to fill my whole body and I would lean in hoping it would never end. Other than the night in the ER after my auto accident, it had been since I was a child that I had experienced that version of my Dad. Why did he choose to shut down, ignore, find fault, turn his back and reject?

I had now become strong enough not to put myself in that pain any longer.

Ten years went by without seeing my Dad. Other than the occasional cordial phone call, we were not in each other's lives. I continued to feel indifferent towards him. I didn't feel hatred, I didn't really feel anything.

As I moved through my thirties and into my forties, I still struggled to know who I was. More career changes within my industry were chosen because I was searching for something. Uncertain of what that "something" might be. I switched Salons more than once, I stepped into positions to later regret my decisions. My early 40s brought my first orthopedic surgery... A hip replacement due to severe arthritis caused from that terrible car accident some twenty years earlier. I would later go on to have my other hip done and eventually both of my knees. Physical pain coupled with a physical career equals a whole lot of agony. Orthopedic surgeries bring tough recoveries, making moving a whole new challenge. My stubborn independence made it very difficult to rely on others. Each time I underwent surgery, in addition to my brother, Lee Anne was always there. She was at the hospital, she talked to the doctors, she stayed with me for several days after, and at times had to even help me out of bed. I relied on her not just as a friend, but as family.

Her daughter Terra grows into a beautiful woman. She gets married, and eventually becomes the mother of three adorable children. Watching her dedication to her family is inspiring. I was honored to be asked to speak at her wedding and years later, was invited to be god-mother to her youngest. I love her and her family like a Mom would. My magical bond with her brother Chase has stayed just as firm as the day he was born. Watching him grow up through elementary school and then into high school, playing sports, going to college, embarking on relationships... He's close with both of his parents, but he and I have always shared something a little extra special. That toddler expression of him laying on the floor and jumping to open the door as fast as he can when he sees me through the window is the way I feel every time I get to spend a little time with him.

My friendships and relationships are everything to me and the circle of close friends I have been fortunate to build around me have substituted well where family hasn't been present. They say you can't pick your family, but you can choose your friends... and I have chosen very well.

Self-reflection was uncovering themes and patterns I noticed and so often I saw myself reacting before I chose whether or not to react that way. Protect first, analyze later.

The thick, enormous wall I built around me for protection has worked well keeping me from harm, yet as much as I would like to crawl over and breathe on the other side, I had no idea where to even start.

# Happy Birthday!

In the summer of 2011, my 47th birthday was approaching. I was currently working at Lee Anne's large salon and day spa and in addition to doing hair, I also served as director of education teaching both technical and interpersonal classes for the large salon staff. Although I thoroughly enjoyed working there for 4 and 1/2 years, I was now craving the solitude and control of having my own home salon again.

Back in 2001, a year after buying my home I had created my own studio space in my lower level that I operated with success for just over 6 years, but closed in the middle of 2007 when the housing market went bust along with predictions of soaring inflation. Out of fear, I closed my small business and instead, sought security in a larger environment. Going to work for my best friend was no doubt a gamble, but Lee Anne welcomed me with open arms and I enjoyed doing what I could to impact others to grow in their talents. After a hand full of years, I began craving a more peaceful environment again and I was dreaming up a better version than the first time around of my in-home full service salon.

As I strategically created lists of supplies and purchases I would need to reopen my Salon, I came up with the minimum amount of $1800 to get things off the ground. At the time, I did not have $1800 so, the dream remained inside. As I reached into my mailbox one day, I retrieved my yearly birthday card from Dad. He was always punctual with the card arriving a few days before my birthday. As I opened it, a piece of paper fell onto the floor. It appeared to be the back of a check. He didn't normally send money. If he did, it was $20 or so, but as I turned the check over I saw it was written out for $2000! I was in complete shock! I actually called him right away to ask if he meant to send me $20... Or maybe $200? I couldn't believe this was correct. Dad assured me that it was indeed intentional. He and his wife had done some maneuvering of their finances and decided to bless their children. Her five kids and his two each got a little money. There was no way he could have known what my needs were because I didn't speak it aloud to anyone.

Yet, there it was! Now I can re-open my home salon! I had no reason not to. So I did! I reassembled the salon equipment. I painted the walls and added new decor. I reinstated my salon license. It was all a lot of work, but I was driven to see it all come alive.

My salon re-opened on November 1, 2011 and it has been a success everyday since. A carefully chosen clientele to fill my schedule. The ability to have just a flight of stairs for a daily commute. Creating the perfect environment to welcome my clients into. Choosing just the right coffee to serve and background music to play. When my gift of creativity is nestled in with my strong work ethic, I am at my best. Since Dad was so instrumental in helping me, I kept him in the loop as I was pursuing along the way. He seemed genuinely interested and happy for me, and we were chatting more than ever before. I was cautious not to get my hopes up, but quite honestly, I enjoyed this new attention. Right around this same time, I was also involved in a class at my church that dealt with resolving family issues. During our discussion time, the people who sat at my table heard about this development, and they encouraged me to enter in. Over the years, Dad and June had invited me to come down to visit numerous times. I had avoided it for a whole decade, but now I was actually considering taking the chance to go see them. In spring of 2012 I got on a plane and nervously flew down to visit them. Although worried I would be disappointed, the hope of something different overshadowed my concern. By now, Dad and June had moved back to Dad's home town of Columbia, South Carolina. They both had family and friends in the area and felt it was a good place to live out their years. My plane landed and the two of them picked me up at the airport. I had seen my Dad show warmth and excitement showcased to others but, now it was being expressed to me! Arriving at their home for the first time, the environment was very different. Dad was different… He was still himself and who I was used to, but, there was a softness about him. He didn't disagree with my every word. He didn't criticize my looks, actions, or ways. But instead, seemed to welcome my presence. He actually listened to what I had to say, and seemed to enjoy my input. I could not have been any more surprised to see this change. I came back for another visit in the fall, and the following year flew down to spend the holidays. It had been many years since we had spent Christmas together, but it was clear they were both excited to have me.

Dad's ultimate favorite pastime was watching movies. He could sit for hours and watch them back-to-back. Dad would carefully pick out movies meaningful to him that he wanted to share. Always a man of few words, it was kind of his love language. One afternoon he and I were sitting side-by-side in their giant recliners watching a movie. I saw movement out of the corner of my eye, and as I looked down, I see Dad's arm stretched out and hand reaching in my direction. Initially I was confused, wondering what he was doing. I searched up to his eyes to which stared straight at the screen, and then I realized... He wants to hold my hand! This was so out of character and for one second, I hesitated. My feelings were conflicted. The thought came to mind... Where was this affection my whole life? But, I took Dad's hand and he squeezed my fingers between his very tightly. He couldn't always say how he felt but with this gesture, he didn't have to say a word. His hand squeeze said what he could not.

Our visits continued. Those conversations grew deeper and our hugs lasted a little bit longer. I would go see them in early spring and then again in late fall spending about a weeks time. It was so shocking to me how our relationship grew over the next few years. Saying goodbye actually brought tears rather than relief. That closeness would translate to our phone calls once I was home. Dad would follow up with me about things we had shared. And, he began sharing himself with me. Reminiscing about his childhood, Marine Corps service, and college days. I loved listening to his stories about life in the deep south with his parents he so loved and his brothers who he looked up to. He shared with me a story of his childhood where food was scarce and there wasn't always enough to go around. After feeding her boys, his mother would wrap up a biscuit and put it aside because she knew that in the middle of the night, one of those little boys of hers would wake her up, complaining that his tummy was still hungry. She would get up, pour a little milk and honey on that biscuit to soften it and feed it to her son. Sometimes, it was Dad who ate the leftover biscuit while his mother sat and waited. He pondered, *"How many times did she go to bed hungry while putting a little aside, sacrificing for her sons?"* I was getting to know a different man and my heart was gravitating to him more and more as my guard diminished. He and I were on a new journey. It was so unexpected! So long overdue.

# DNA

The website, ancestry.com had been around for a while and I was aware of it and how it helped people assemble their family trees. In 2013 they introduced a form of DNA testing to uncover one's heritage and ethnicity. The limited information I received upon turning 18 in regards to my adoption, shared that my birth mother was of Scottish descent, but the information on my birth father yielded the term "Unknown." Throughout my life, people would constantly ask me what nationality I was. I was guessed to be everything from Spanish, Greek, Italian, etc. I would joke with people that their guess was as good as mine... and reminded them not to make any ethnic jokes because, they just "might" offend me.

I ordered my kit and sent my DNA in to be analyzed, excited to see what my results would be. A few weeks later I received the confirmation that I was in fact 48% Scottish. But, the surprise of my life came when I discovered that I'm also 24% indigenous/ Mexican, 17% Spanish, with bits of western and south European including sprinkles of Portuguese, Basque, Senegalese, Cameroon, and Eastern Bantu. I shared these findings with Dad and he found them to be so interesting as well...The Mexican neighbor lady who used to call me her "little Juanita" nailed it! For days, I'd dissect my pie chart and researched the different countries and areas listed to get a glimpse of the culture and people that make up my heritage. Finally! An answer to my life long question. I was more than thrilled to have this information and the days that followed gave me a reason to stand a little taller and hold my head up a little straighter.

What I did not know, was that in addition to my ethnic pie chart, I was also connected to others who shared my DNA. Relatives! Blood relatives!!

As I scrolled through my matches, I would zoom in on everyone's face where a picture was provided. Most of these people were distant cousins, but still, my first glimpse of blood relatives.

The great majority had Mexican surnames. I would say my first name next to theirs to see what it sounded like. Which one of these names was mine?

Since I knew the Scottish piece was from my birth-Mom, I could guesstimate which relatives were on her side and which were on my birth-Dad's.

In my excitement, I sent a few messages through the site to see if some of these matches could help me to identify either of my birth-parents. But, without knowing their names or any real identifying information, nothing came of it. Some of the people were very eager to help and tried to think of family members matching my descriptions but, nothing definitive came my way. Every handful of months or so I would check again to see if there were any new DNA matches. I'd get excited again and send more messages. Still… nothing. Then, on September 19, 2016 I received a "first cousin" DNA match. This was the closest match I had received so far. In a hurry, I sent this gentleman relative with the username "La Familia" the following message…

*"Hello, according to ancestry.com we are very likely first cousins! This is the closest DNA match I have seen so far. I am adopted and know nothing about my birth-parents… Which is why I sent DNA to get an ethnic profile. I am curious as to what your story is. I believe you would be related to me on my birth-father's side. It would be wonderful to hear back from you.*
*Barbara"*

For weeks I checked for his returned message but, my inbox stayed empty.

# We're Just Getting Started

In October 2016 I flew down to spend a week visiting Dad and June. By now, our visits had become regular and expected. Awkwardness and uncomfortableness were now gone. This time when I got there, Dad complained that his back was a little sore. In getting the guest room ready, he decided the mattress needed to be flipped over before fresh sheets made up the bed for my visit. I scolded him for doing such a physical chore at his rich age of 87 but, he downplayed it, convinced his pain would pass. I'll admit that I was flattered at the gesture…that he went so out of his way. The man who turned his back to me for decades was now prepping for my visit and welcoming me with the simple act of a mattress flip.

After my trip and back home in Minnesota, the day before Thanksgiving June called to tell me Dad had been rushed to the hospital. His recent backache had gotten much worse, and he was not able to get up out of his chair. The next day we discovered he had bone cancer. Apparently it was a residual affect of the prostate cancer he had overcome some 25 years ago. It had now metastasized to his pelvis and spine and was growing rapidly. Our phone calls were daily now, and I could hear his voice weakening as the weeks followed. I was planning a trip to go see him in early spring as usual, but it was clear to me that he might not be on this earth by then. He was declining rapidly, and once hospice entered into the picture, I knew it was a race against time. I changed my plans and arranged to go down sooner but his decline was so severe I was concerned it still wouldn't be soon enough to see him again.

The ache in my heart was so overwhelming, and it took all the strength I had to get through my days in a semi-normal fashion. All I could think about was, I finally had the Dad I knew was there all along. The relationship I so desired since I was a little child on his lap in front of the TV was now the reality we were living. His acknowledgment turned in my direction, willingly and lovingly. I begged God… *"Please! Let him live longer! We're just getting started."*

On a Saturday evening on my way to church, my phone rang. It was an unfamiliar number with a South Carolina area code. I figured I should answer it and was quite surprised to find that it was my Dad's hospice nurse. As I sat in my car in the church parking lot, the kindest woman with a thick, southern accent greeted me on the phone.

*"Honey, I'm your Daddy's hospice nurse...now, I'm not supposed to do this, but I just had to get a hold of you to tell you what's been going on with your Daddy!"*

She spoke with such urgency... I knew from her tone that she was in a horrible position to tell me all she shared. Dad's pain medication that hospice had provided had been stolen by June's son. Along with his meds, her son exited the state in my Dad's car. Dad was too sick and weak to do anything about it and, assuming that after Dad's death, anything he owned would obviously go to his wife, his stepson thought he would take his inheritance early in the form of Dad's car. Dad had owned many cars in his lifetime. He always took immaculate care of them. Once retired, keeping his car clean and perfect became his new hobby. You could eat off of his floor mats. Other than a moderate savings account and a few investments, the car was really all Dad had and he wanted to leave it to his kids. What his wife's son did not understand was that June and Dad had a prenup. Her belongings and assets would go to her five children and his would go to his two. It was not his stepson's car to take, but with a history of drug abuse and addiction, stealing the drugs and the car were not a total surprise. Thankfully, Dad's hospice nurse was able to secure more drugs to combat Dad's intense pain. There he laid in a hospital bed, weak and vulnerable. He did not want his kids to know any of this for fear of worrying us. I will always be so grateful to that nurse for digging up my phone number and calling me.

I might have spent a whole decade not seeing my Dad, but for my brother, it had been at least two decades. Their relationship had diminished to infrequent emails, and even less frequent phone calls.

I always saw them as so close… For many years, my brother could do no wrong in my Dad's eyes. He was the son he wanted, and it showed. As time passed, their differences grew bigger. They did not share views on religion or politics, or just about anything else. Their conversations would often get heated, to which was good reason to stop communicating. As I drove home, relaying these details from Dad's hospice nurse to my brother over the phone, I could not control my anger. The language that came out of my mouth hardly reflected the fact that I had just been at church. He agreed with me that the situation was horrible and needed to be rectified. My poor brother had to listen to me on the phone call after call crying my eyes out, telling him I could not go down there and take care of it alone and pleading with him to go with me.

Understandably, he was reluctant, but with my begging, his wife's encouragement and use of their Delta miles, the two of us got on a plane two days later. Throughout our journey, we were in constant communication with June's daughter who had driven down to be of help. She was caring for Dad when the hospice nurses couldn't be there and being a support to her Mother. Because of limited access, we had to fly into Charlotte, North Carolina and then rent a car to drive the almost 2 hours to Dad's home in Columbia.

It was uncertain whether or not we were going to get there in time and we were racing against the clock as the text messages about Dad's worsening condition didn't give us much hope. As we pulled into the driveway, my heart beating so fast, it was all I could do to calm myself and put on a semblance of normalcy to great Dad. We got inside the house and made our way to the back den where they had made a room for Dad. I had just been to visit less than three months earlier, and yet, I hardly recognized Dad. His color was so pale. He was skin and bones. His thinning hair, even thinner and now, the consistency of chick fur. His eyes were sunken in and his cheeks so hollow. As we entered the room, June and her daughter left to give us some privacy. He looked up at us with so much intention… so patiently waiting for this moment. As I approached him, relief shown in his eyes. After my embrace and kiss, he searched with eagerness in the other direction to look for his son. With diminished strength, he firmly reached his hand out to offer a man's handshake. As their hands embraced, he looked my brother in the eye and said with such humility, *"It's been a long time..."* I saw my brother's face soften as he looked back in Dad's eyes and agreed *"yes it has."* *"You look good!"* Dad whispered, his voice so raspy. His son smiled patting his midsection, *"Well, maybe with a few extra pounds and less hair..."* Dad just stared at him and repeated *"you look good."* 20 years gone, like it was nothing. Dad's handshake showed my brother respect, and I think it surprised him.

We stayed in town for a full week with many tasks in front of us. First on the list… Sitting down with June to talk about her son taking Dad's car. I was so proud of my brother and how he handled the situation. With patience and respect, he gently told June that before the week was over, she needed to convey to her son that the car was to be returned before we left. If not, we had secured his address and we would call the authorities and report the car stolen. Neither one of us really cared about the car itself but, we knew how important it was to Dad. June was mortified by her sons actions and was more than compliant. Decades of enabling his addictions made it next to impossible for her to be strict with him. With us taking the bull by the horns, she could have the relief of just being the messenger.

It felt so good to sit at Dad's bedside, letting him know that we knew the whole situation, and what we had done to remedy it. My brother patting Dad's arm telling him, *"We've got your back Dad."* Dad's surprised look melted into understanding. He nodded and actually gave us a small smile to show his gratitude. Next on the list was securing all of Dad's pain medication and storing it all in a hidden spot for if and when June's son returned. I put myself in charge of administering Dad's morphine and other medications, keeping a firm schedule. My number one goal was to ease his pain as much as possible. We spent many hours sitting with Dad as he mostly slept, but had moments of lucidity where he so enjoyed seeing our faces. He was no longer eating food, but would ask for lemonade and Pepsi. I'm sure he understood that hydration would help him stay alive for a few more days. My brother and I went to the funeral home and made arrangements.

Working all those years as an electrical engineer, Dad had many nice suits that hung in his closet. We had lots to choose from, but in our search we also discovered Dad's pristine condition, wool Marine Corps dress blues. With Dad now so skinny from his cancer, we commented that his old uniform would actually fit him again! I believe the idea hit us both at the exact same moment... There wasn't much in this world that Dad was more proud of than his service in the Marine Corps, and it seemed only fitting to have him buried in his dress blues.

Each day, Dad got weaker and slept more. His moments of consciousness were fewer and shorter. I slept out on the living room sofa, just 20 feet or so from the room he was sleeping in. At night, I would bring him water and let him know I was there. Thankfully he could still draw from a straw. I helped him position himself to take a drink. I put lotion on his hands that were so dry. By now, I was doing most of the talking, and he would sleep. It was January 31, the night before our flight back home. I sat with him, telling him how happy we both were to spend this time with him. I thanked him for all the things I could think to thank him for. I did not mention all of the things that hurt me. Those things were now in the past. I kept reminding him of the fact that we were leaving the next day. Without actually saying it, I wanted him to know that he could finally let go. I talked to him about heaven... Reassuring him he would get to see his parents and brothers again. Dad and I shared the same faith. He was maybe a bit more legalistic and me, a little more progressive but, we would always find common ground to talk about.

*"Dad, you get to go to a place that is flooded with the most amazing love. A love so enormous that it covers everything. Every doubt, every heartbreak, every failure, every mistake. All the disappointments of*

*this earth will not be there — only love!"* I thought about his time in prison all those years ago and I hoped he had asked God to forgive him...and also that he had forgiven himself.

I told Dad I was actually a little jealous that he gets to go to paradise before me, but reminded him that we would one day be together again to continue our beautiful relationship.
It was now the wee hours of the morning and it had been a long time since Dad had been responsive. I felt that he might want some privacy. My tears were so constant and I'm sure that affected him. As long as I was at his bedside, he wanted to stay strong for me. I told him I was going into the living room to lay down on the sofa for a while, but to just call if he needed me for anything, and I'd come right back. I must have kissed him on his head a hundred times and making sure his bedding was comfortable for him just before I left his side. *"I love you Daddy!"*

Then, for some reason, I said... *"Good night, sleep tight, don't let the bedbugs bite."* At that, his face moved. One eye opened and the side of his mouth curled up into a smile. It lasted but a second — then I knew, he had heard everything. I hadn't said that phrase to my Dad since I was a little girl, but he remembered.

Closing the French doors to the den I completely broke down. No longer able to hold back, I pleaded to God... *"Please, take him tonight!"* I couldn't bear the thought of getting on that plane and leaving him in such a vulnerable state. As much as I wanted him to stay alive for us to continue growing in our relationship that had started so late — more than that, I begged God to take him up and hold him close keeping him safe.

It took quite a while for me to finally fall asleep, but after some time I drifted away, so emotionally exhausted from the weight of my heart. Hours later I woke with the sunlight. No one in the house was up yet. Quietly walking into the den to check on Dad, I slowly opened the French doors and as I saw him, I immediately knew he was gone.

His eyes were actually open, and his arms were fixed in front of his face, almost as if to shield himself from a bright light. I looked up and thanked God, knowing that he was now safe. Checking the garage, his car had been returned in the night. Later that afternoon, my brother and I boarded the plane back home. We would come down a few weeks later to have a proper memorial service for Dad where others who loved him could pay their respects. I was surprised to see so many there. Their handy man's wife with tears told me how much she loved Dad and shared stories of how good he was to their family. I had no idea. Scripture was read, the flag was folded and Taps was played. We hoped it was as humble as he would have wanted.

# From Grief to Gift

I was completely unprepared for the depth of grief I experienced in the weeks and months that followed. I thought about Dad every day. Tears were an hourly occurrence. I suffered colds and flu that whole year more than I had ever experienced in the past. I was exhausted and slept a lot. This loss felt entirely different than losing Mom. This time, there was no sense of relief. The five beautiful years we had built up till now were so significant in reversing the past. Literally, my bones ached for the sound of his voice on the phone. I found myself talking to him all the time. I had no idea if he could hear me but I talked to him nonetheless.

Five months after my message to my DNA relative, on February 28, 2017, 29 days after Dad died, he finally answered.

*"Hello, I'm sorry about not noticing your message. I would definitely like to hear more of our possible relationship. Please contact me."*

I have won the lottery! There was a firework show going on inside me. This was what I needed to interrupt the depth of grief I was lying in. I messaged him back immediately and shared with him what my birth-father's approximate age would be now, along with the other few details I knew. He was originally from Illinois, his occupation was a Machinist, and in the mid-60s he resided in Seattle, Washington. The gentleman relative answered me back stating that this information did not ring a bell with anyone in his family. I wondered... How could this be? If he and I are as closely related as our DNA states, he has to know who my birth-father is. I had no choice, but to accept his answer. Horribly disappointed, I continued to wait.

Several months later, I messaged him again and wondered if time had helped jog his memory. There was no response.

On November 14, 2017 another DNA match appeared on my profile.

Again… a close, first cousin. I quickly messaged her a similar note asking if my description of my birth father resembled any of her male relatives. A couple of days later I heard back from her, letting me know she had an uncle who lived in Washington state who had died earlier that year. I quickly came back, asking for his name and if he had any children I could reach out to. Four months later on March 19, 2018 I finally received a reply?

*"His name was Medina. I talked to my uncles stepdaughter, DeDe and she said you could call her to discuss any help she can provide…"*

Not logging onto my *ancestry.com* profile that day, I had not seen her message.

Instead, DeDe did a search on my name and found a connection to my salon and sent me an email.

13 months after Dad's passing, I am now on the phone on a Monday night talking to DeDe discovering who my birth-Dad was.

My two Dads died just over two months apart. I imagine the both of them meeting in the afterlife. Somehow, instantly knowing who each other was. Maybe a handshake exchange occurred with Dad telling Ruben, *"You fathered a daughter you never knew about, and I raised her."*

I studied the pictures of my birth-Dad as they came to me, zooming in on every detail I could see and soaking up any story I could possibly detect. I so badly wanted to know him. Sometimes, I recognized the emotion he carried in the photos because, my face carried the same expression at times. He's proud in this shot, unsure in another. Laughing his hardest here because, that's how I look when I'm hysterical! His younger pictures gave a sense of humor and a swagger. He was so handsome! As he aged, his eyes carried more humility. Ruben was very fair skinned. Actually, you wouldn't necessarily know he's Mexican at all. DeDe told me for many years he went by the nickname, "Rudy" not wanting people to know his heritage. In my grandmother's attempts to buy groceries for her family, she would often be kicked out of the local grocery store because she was Mexican. Resourceful as she was, she'd hand the grocery list to her oldest son, Ruben and tell him to go shopping because he could pass for white.

Gazing upon his childhood pictures, I see where all my freckles came from.

What stood out about him? What was his essence? His favorite movies, seasons, food? His pet peeves? Ruben, who were you? I so badly want to know everything.

Rueben

Two months later on Memorial Day weekend I flew to Portland, Oregon where DeDe lived. She graciously welcomed me into her home and that weekend, drove me to Seattle to meet family members. By now, she had filled me in on his life's story. He had eight younger siblings, his father left his mother after just under a decade of marriage and two kids. She remarried and had seven more children. Relations with his stepfather were not good, with him leaving home and joining the Air Force… lying about his age being he wasn't old enough to enlist. He was stationed in Washington state where he trained as a Machinist and worked in that field throughout the rest of his life. A brief stint with Boeing landed him in Seattle, where he met and married his wife. She brought with her two small daughters from a previous marriage, and they soon had one of their own. Ruben only fathered one child or, so he thought. Becoming a stepfather did not come easy to him and apparently, the first five years of marriage were pretty rocky. He and his wife would split up, get back together and split up again. It was during this time that he discovered my birth-mother. He was 29 in the fall of 1963 and according to his pictures, was very good looking. His younger photos showcased a smile that I'm certain could charm just about anyone. Ruben met my birth-Mom at a dance hall in late October or early November. They only saw each other a couple of times, but, it was enough for me to enter into the picture. Afterwards, he returned to his wife and family. As far as I know, he never knew about me. I was the result of infidelity. I can feel my birth-Mom's agony, discovering that she was pregnant after Ruben had quickly exited the picture.

Now in Seattle, I was on my way to meet my niece and her family, my nephew, and DeDe's youngest daughter. They would tell me all about their grandpa, a.k.a. "Bumpa." We were all gathering at his house where I was also about to meet my birth-Dad's wife of over 50 years. The woman he cheated on to which I am here. I told DeDe that if she didn't want to meet me that I totally understood. In fact, I expected it. But she assured me that when her mother was made aware of my existence, she wasn't surprised, deep down knowing her husband was not always faithful. She told her family, *"We're going to be nice to her… It wasn't her fault."*

As we drove into the neighborhood, I was so taken by the beauty and variety of rhododendrons blooming everywhere! As the car pulled up, my Dad's widow came out onto her front doorstep. Before I could say a word, she put her arms out wide waving me in. My heart skipped! As I walked up to her, she embraced me with so much warmth and acceptance. After our long hug, holding onto my shoulders she backed away, looked at me and said *"YOU are Ruben's daughter! Without a doubt."* We spent the afternoon visiting and taking photos. Looking at my niece and nephew was my first experience seeing blood relatives in the flesh. A moment I had fantasized about my whole life. I didn't really see a resemblance with my nephew, but my niece shared my dark hair, brown eyes and freckles. Their mother, my half-sister was not there. I have not met her. Maybe someday... While in his home I felt a sense of familiarity. Almost as if I had been there before but, clearly knowing I had not. As I was shown around, I asked if I could use the bathroom and was pointed to the nearest one. *"Here, use Dad's bathroom."* I closed the door and looked around noticing very little looked like it had changed in the year since he had passed. I wondered, is his DNA still present in this room? I'll admit, I opened the medicine cabinet and looked in the vanity drawer, searching for something that belong to him. Something personal... Not that I was going to take anything, but I just wanted to touch it, being that I had missed the opportunity to touch him.

My birth-Dad supported his family by being one of only two men in the country who was trained and certified to sell, assemble and instruct operators to use one of the first hydraulic metal crushing machines. They were often used in junkyards and car lots to crush old cars into scrap metal. The family moved around quite a bit with his job, but eventually settled back into their favorite spot outside Seattle, Washington. There they had land, horses, and other animals. Most of his pictures show him as a working man. Often in blue jeans and a work shirt with tousled hair and a look of determination. I missed out on the opportunity to meet him by less than one year. But the pictures — all the pictures... I couldn't get enough of them! I would look at the date they were taken and immediately get a picture in my mind's eye of myself at that time. I couldn't help but interject my appearance into the photo through my imagination and wonder…How might I have been his little girl? How might he have been a father to me? I wondered if his view of me would have instilled a better self image? I learned that when his daughter was turning 15, he wanted her to have a Quinceañera, to which she was not at all interested in. When reading about it's meaning, I innately knew that I would've eaten it up!

After my trip to Seattle, DeDe and her sister Cindy stayed in close contact with me. They told me about their great memories throughout the years of visiting all of Dad's huge family in the Quad Cities. Sharing such sweet stories of their grandmother — my grandmother too. These relatives were intrigued to find out about me and we all planned a trip that summer to have a family reunion. I could hardly wait for the day to come.

I drove the five plus hours south excited and nervous. Checking into the hotel, I looked to my right at the woman checking in at the next console. Instinctively, I knew she was a relative! And she was! My first cousin who provided my Dad's name. As I met cousin after cousin, an aunt and several uncles, I kept seeing my eyes appearing on other's faces. He has my eyes… So does she… For the first time in my life, I saw glimpses of myself in others. With several of these relatives, I felt almost an immediate bond. A connection as if we had always known each other. This was a first for me. Growing up in my dysfunctional home, I longed to be with people who made me feel received, appreciated, and understood. Might this be that opportunity? DeDe, Cindy and I stayed for a full week. We shared a hotel room in town and by the end of the week, I felt like their younger sister. We had many gatherings and outings with the family. On the second day, we all bordered a trolley car and went on a tour, stopping at all the houses our grandmother lived in where they had spent their childhood years. We stopped at the cemetery where she was buried and found her marker. As I looked upon her stone, I was surprised to see that she had died on my birthday. Without really thinking, I said it out loud to which brought an interesting reaction from the family. They seemed to think it was a sign from her! One thing all of the cousins had in common was their love for their grandmother. The stories of her cooking amazing food and caring for them in her home were beautiful! I have no doubt that she would've called me her "nieta" and poured out that love for me as well.

**My Grandparents,**
**Delores Medina and Ester Leon-Medina on their wedding day**

After finishing at the cemetery, we stopped at a Mexican bakery to buy Conchas, a Mexican sweet bread. They were all shocked I had never had it before. Up until just a few years ago, I didn't even know I was Mexican! Although my Mom was an excellent cook, she never cooked Mexican food nor did we go out for it. I don't think it was something my family appreciated. As a kid, I loved going to the neighbors for dinner. The Delarosa's and the Perez's cooked amazing Mexican food. Now I know why I loved it so much.

Throughout the week, I spent time with so many cousins and most of my uncles, as well as my one remaining aunt. A common story I heard from more than one of them was about how Ruben loved to get gussied up and go out dancing. In his younger days he was known to hit the dance floor whenever Chubby Checker's The Twist was played. One of my birth-Dad's cousins told me, *"He could really get that leg up there!"* I have seen The Twist danced many times on old TV shows and I don't quite recall a high leg move but, I giggled, wondering how he might have improvised.

In the fall of 2016, the squamous cell skin cancer that Ruben had successfully treated years before, had come back and metastasized to other parts of his body. He was sick, and the clock was ticking. Many of Ruben's relatives told me stories of him making phone calls — to check in and to make amends. Some of these relatives hadn't talked to him in a very long time but were touched to hear from him. Ruben carried the pain of being an unwanted stepchild. Throughout his life, that pain caused him to act out at times, making some of his relationships very difficult. My heart goes out to him hearing about his efforts to right those wrongs before he left this earth. In the eyes and voices of his grandchildren, I can see how greatly he was loved and adored. I picture that in his nature now, as I hold a part of him too.

We took so many group photos during that week. Looking back at them, I heard one of my cousins remark, *"You can tell who the spouses are because they're the white ones."* Everyone laughed, and I remarked, *"I'm white."* To which my cousins looked at me, smiled at each other, then laughed nodding their heads. *"No you're not."* So many awakenings happened during that week.

On my last day in town, DeDe, Cindy and I went out for breakfast with my uncle Leonard and his family. By now, I realized that he was "La Familia," the username of the first DNA match I was communicating with early on. As we left the restaurant and walked through the parking lot, he asked me to come to the car with him because he had something for me. He gave me a couple of gifts…

Some things that belonged to his mother — my grandmother. *"You have my mother's eyes."* He told me. As we stood there by ourselves, with tears in his eyes and with genuine sincerity, he apologized for not answering my messages. *"I was new on ancestry.com and thought that maybe I was being scammed. Im so sorry... if I had answered your message back then, you might have met your Dad. He was still alive then."*

As much as my heart broke with the truth of his statement, I was also well aware that if he HAD told my birth-Dad about me, it was very likely that Ruben would have shut the whole thing down. Not wanting his wife to know that he had cheated on her all those years ago. And, THAT potential rejection would have been more than I could bare.

I told Uncle Leonard that it all might have been for the best the way things played out, and as much as I would have loved to have met Ruben, I'm so happy to have met his family — my family.

He shared with me that when my grandmother was a little girl, she and her family had to flee during the Mexican Revolution. Her father, my great grandfather was falsely accused of sharing information and being a spy against Mexico. A noose was actually placed around his neck, and they threaten to execute him. My great grandmother begged and pleaded with them to spare his life. They eventually released him and with only what they could fit on a wagon, they fled the land that they owned... leaving it all behind. Eventually they were able to build a new life for themselves in America to which their resilient legacy lives on within this whole family.

**My Great-Great-Grandfather Leocadio Mendoza and his daughter, my Great-Grandmother, Concepción Mendoza**

As I headed north for the almost 6 hour drive home, I found myself smiling without even realizing it. Mile after mile my heart felt so light... so full of life! What a gift after experiencing the heavy grief of losing Dad the year before. I imagined coming back for holidays or just a visit. I was filled with hope that those relationships would grow and deepen. I was fortunate to have my newfound Michigan cousins come to my home for the following Thanksgiving. And, less than a year later, traveled with another cousin to visit DeDe, who was living in Hawaii at the time.

On that first visit to Washington, DeDe had said to me, *"You should change your last name to Medina!"* I couldn't help but laugh to myself because the irony was...growing up, my brother used to say to me, *"You're so lucky you're a girl! You'll get married someday and get a*

*different last name! I am stuck with this name for the rest of my life!"*
Our last name was Reddick…RED DICK! The jokes we both had
hurled at us over the years! My brother of course, getting the worst of
it… Red-dick, blue-dick, green-dick, purple-dick… I have to admit,
Medina sounded so much better! On March 20th 2019, exactly one
year and one day after finding out about my birth-Dad, I went to the
downtown Minneapolis courthouse and had my last name legally
changed to Medina. A cousin from Iowa flew in to be a witness and
to celebrate with me. No disrespect intended towards Norman and
Marion, but taking back something that belonged to me felt so right.

Today, I communicate with Cindy and DeDe frequently. We might
not be blood related, but I can honestly say, we are family. I regularly
check in with my Michigan cousins, and Uncle Leonard AKA "La
Familia" and I continue to keep tabs on each other. Social media
allows me to keep up with the rest of them. These relatives never
asked me to come out of the woodwork yet, they were very gracious
to welcome me, filling me in on so much of my family's history. I
realistically can't ask for more. Most of the people I know rarely
interact with their cousins. I guess that's pretty normal. Nonetheless,
I am thrilled to know where I come from. Knowing the rich history
of my beautiful, Mexican ancestors and the challenges they have
conquered fills me with pride! And the strength that they carried, I
can feel running through my veins as well.

# Lightening Strikes Twice!

In the fall of 2019, I get a hit on my *23andMe* account — a second cousin DNA match, Cheryl messaged me sharing she had been hard at work putting together family tree information and, stumbling upon our connection, was baffled to who I was. She asked me many questions that I had no idea how to answer. I knew she was related to me on my maternal side so, I shared with her that I was given up for adoption at birth, and knew very little about who my birth-mother was. I provided her approximate age, along with a few other details that I was aware of. She came back intrigued and over the next several weeks, we emailed each other many times, as she seemed to be on a mission to discover who my birth-Mom was. Early on, she pondered...

*"The age best matches my cousin Heather but, it couldn't be her. She never married, nor had any children."*

When I read this, I innately knew it was her. Never marrying, nor having children somehow confirmed it in my heart, because that was my path as well. How else am I just like her? Cheryl shared this news with the rest of her family, and they all agreed that it could NOT be Heather. Convinced that if a pregnancy and birth had occurred, they'd know about it. They asked me to gather more proof. This was very challenging, due to the circumstances to which adoptions were conducted in the 60s with records being sealed and no identifying information being shared. I registered online through the Los Angeles County Bureau of Adoptions and requested any further information I was legally privy too. Apparently, with the explosion of the databases ancestry.com and 23andMe, they were flooded with requests. I waited a year and four months to hear back from them. Once I did, I shared a few significant details with Heather's family. She lived in Southern California. She had one brother. She would've been 21 years old when she gave birth to me. She worked at the time as a "girl Friday." She enjoyed writing and liked raising tropical fish. These details, along with other information about where she lived and grew up confirmed that it was indeed, Heather. She apparently hid her pregnancy from everyone, and took her secret to the grave. Sadly, Heather had died several years earlier at the age of 60 from Cholangiocarcinoma — a rare cancer found in the bile duct of the liver. During this time, one of my favorite long standing clients, Scott who happened to be a huge ancestry buff... successfully putting together family trees for both he and his wife's family, was in for his monthly haircut. He had figured out how to use the information that ancestry.com offered to dig up results. I would share these stories with him when he came in and he was always so intrigued. He asked me, *"Have you seen a picture of her yet?"* I had not, nor did I know how to go about finding one. By now, I had done my share of googling her name again and again but, nothing other than previous addresses came up. Scott was pretty confident. *"Give me 24 hours and I will find you a photo!"* *"You're on Scott!"*

I woke the next morning to my usual routine of feeding my Pugs and making coffee. Mustang, my boy with his brindle coat and golden brown eyes was my velcro dog, and had my heart from the second I picked him up. Three years later I got his companion, Valentine. A traditional fawn color with her velvet-like black ears and perfect diamond shape on her head. She was named after the day I brought her home. Mustang let Valentine think she was in charge but, she followed him everywhere. The runt of her litter and extra tiny but, full of sass and a total diva!

Checking email on my phone, I see Scott has sent me something. "Picture" read in the subject line. He did it! And it didn't even take him 24 hours!!

I feel the weight of what's in front of me, and I nervously moved to sit down. I opened the email and there she was! Her picture jumped off my phone and startled me. Again, how do you recognize a face you've never seen before? I looked more like her than I did Ruben. And, I looked a lot like Ruben! It was her high school graduation photo. So young and fresh with the world at her feet. Her hair color and texture, her lips and smile, they were all mine. Looking at her picture took my breath away, and I literally felt like I was going to faint.

**Heather's High School Graduation Photo**

Staring at her photo for hours, I couldn't get enough...My eyes had waited a long time to gaze upon her face and I couldn't do anything but soak her in... I had to start work at noon and was struggling to get ready, moving about in complete shock. Getting into the shower, her image is now burned in my brain. I couldn't picture anything else. Physically, I didn't feel right. I began breathing hard...then harder. It's almost like I was hyperventilating and couldn't quite calm myself down. I reached out to hold onto the towel bar in front of me and out of nowhere, I screamed!! It came from my toes, all the way up through my legs, hips, stomach, heart, and arms, I screamed loud and long! Crying out loud to the picture in my head! *"YOU WERE SUPPOSED TO BE MINE!!! And, I was supposed to be yours."*

I held onto that towel bar sobbing and screaming for quite some time. It was so out of character for me and I'm still shocked by it. I certainly didn't choose to respond this way. I'm anything but a tantrum thrower. But, there was something inside me overriding my will. Somehow, I mustered the strength to get myself together and work on clients all day. The weeks that followed brought their share of despair, as I processed who my birth-mother was.

# If Just for a Moment?

I must have read through the paperwork that the Bureau of Adoptions sent me dozens of times. I read the social worker's assessment of my birth-mother. I read my birth-mother's answers to their questions. I read her description of how she met Ruben at a dance. He was approximately eight years older than she was and unbeknownst to her, was a married man. She described him as being charming and very handsome. Did he break out his twist moves to impress her? One of the statements included in the report was, *"Your birth-mother never wavered in her decision to relinquish you."*

Reading this sentence felt like a punch square in my face. Realistically, I know she had no choice. In the mid 60s, being a single mother was not at all an option. Especially raising a child born out of wedlock by a man she barely knew. If she was going to have a chance for a successful life, she had no choice but to give me up for adoption. As much as my reasoning mind could understand this, my heart so badly hoped for a love story. Was there any love in her heart for me, or was our nine months together a reminder of a dreadful memory she couldn't wait to get rid of? The report claimed I stayed in the hospital and didn't go into foster care until 16 days after my birth. In those years, women remained in the hospital for a couple of weeks to mend their body's after giving birth. Did she walk down to the nursery to take a glimpse of me? Or better yet, did she hold me? I will never know. By now I have received many photos of her. This report also provided adequate proof to her relatives who had been in denial due to the fact that Heather kept it a secret, never sharing it with anyone. Thankfully, they were now generous with information and photos. Just like with Ruben, I would scour picture after picture, zooming in and studying every aspect of her expression — wondering if my memory was held by her, and if so, was there any love? For some unrelenting reason it was so important for me to know the answer to this question. For months, I labored with this. By now, self-loathing had walked beside me for decades. I questioned, has this been with me since birth? Or even before? In all honesty, I can't remember a time it hasn't been riding just under the current and spreading to the deepest part of me. Out of desperation, I began seeing a therapist. The dark thoughts were coming constantly like big waves over my head, making treading water more difficult... Each hour, every day, and I felt like I was drowning.

Identifying my birth-parents, and discovering who they were brought insight, but the grief over what might have been was just too much to bare. How might things have been different if I would've had the true love of either of my birth-parents? Sitting with this question woke up so many memories of my growing up years — the reality of my childhood, and how I struggled so to get through it. Somehow, the weight of it all has rendered me incapable of accomplishing dreams that were hoped for. To experience self-worth. To have the support and love of a husband. To be a mother — instinctively knowing that I would have been a very good one. Loosing the opportunity to pour my love into them was grief as tough as I've ever felt. And now more than ever before, I'm realizing it. Why have these dreams evaded me? And why did I forever reject their possibility? My attention was focused on the notion that I should never have come to be. If the brief union between Ruben and Heather hadn't produced my existence, there would have been undoubtedly less pain and sorrow in Heather's life. And I wouldn't have had those early traumatic experiences leading to a childhood of walking on eggshells almost every minute of every day. I wouldn't be the ripe age of 50-something despising myself and stuck in a life not able to realize true love and lasting peace. After Dad's death, I spoke with him all the time. In fact, I still do. Talking to him brings comfort, and somehow lets me know he's with me in spirit. I started having similar conversations with Heather. Telling her all about the sorrow that my heart was carrying, and asking her... Was there any love? Even if just for a moment?

How I prayed...constantly asking God to relieve this despair. I threw myself into leading Bible studies at my home, where I invited women friends to come and explore…what is God saying to us about rejection, disappointment, forgiveness? These studies worked as fuel for me to tread the difficult current but, the waves kept coming and my prayers for rescue were not answered.

On a Sunday afternoon, I was cleaning my kitchen with my earbuds in listening to my Prince playlist. This list is my longest with so much of his music in my catalog. His music has always hit a chord in me that brings me up a level. As I clean and sing along, abruptly the song playing ends and another one begins. I questioned, what was this? At first the music didn't register. I knew it definitely was not Prince so, I grab my phone to look at the screen. It was This Woman's Work by Kate Bush playing. It had been maybe four or five years since I had listened to this song, and my first instinct was to swipe up and go back to Prince. But something strongly stopped me, and I knew I needed to sit down and listen.

The lyrics in the second verse and chorus hit me like a ton of bricks.

*give me these moments back*
*give them back to me*
*give me that little kiss*
*give me your hand.*

*I should be crying but I just can't let it show.*
*I should be hoping but I can't stop thinking*
*of all the things we should've said that we're never said*
*all the things we should've done that we never did*
*all the things that you needed from me*
*all the things that you wanted for me*
*all the things that I should've given but I didn't.*
*Oh darling make it go away*
*just make it go away now.*

I sat hunched over in the chair with my face in my hands completely bawling. Why did my playlist change? Especially to a song that hadn't been pulled up in years. I was pretty done-in for the rest of that day. But I couldn't help but wonder… is this how she felt? And if she did, there was pain over my loss. And often where there's pain, there is love.

By mid March, COVID-19 had invaded our world and the Minnesota State Board required me to stop working for the next 11 weeks. Stress about making ends meet made the waters even rougher to which the treading got harder. Following that, the death of George Floyd and all the trauma that came with it. Civil unrest brought the constant sound of sirens and helicopters flying overhead throughout the summer of 2020. The city I lived in was underwater too. These life events on top of what I was already carrying were a tipping point. As much as I wanted to, I could not tread water with my hands so full. As the weeks turned into months, my mental health hovered in a place of functioning for others to witness but, I knew that I was in trouble. I neglected my health. All my life, my weight fluctuated up and down and now I'm at my heaviest. Deep down, I welcome a heart attack or stroke to bring freedom. My added weight made my knee with the shattered kneecap from my auto accident, now full of arthritis swell and ache after working on my feet all day. The pain was excruciating and after years of Cortisone shots, I could not avoid a knee replacement any longer.

During the lengthy recovery time, another life preserver was thrown my way. Up until now, all I really knew about my birth-Mom was what was in that report. A few details about her interests and hobbies, family, ethnicity, and some health info. With more of her relatives finally excepting that I am in fact her daughter, they started to open up to me and share even more about her. I spent one afternoon with my knee on ice propped up on the sofa talking to a first cousin. He was Heather's beloved nephew Andrew who all the family agreed, he knew her the best. They had enjoyed a close relationship for many years…spending time with each other exploring state parks, interesting dining experiences, shopping excursions, and long talks. For over three hours on speaker phone, he and his partner Eric shared descriptions, stories, and experiences of her that changed what was a black-and-white, one dimensional view of her into a brightly colored scene with depth and elevation — and even a musical score to back it.

She loved spending a random Saturday in a fun part of town checking out interesting shops and eating dim sum at her favorite lunch place. She enjoyed driving along the Pacific Coast Highway in her older model Mercedes convertible wearing her big sun glasses and blasting Bohemian Rhapsody out the speakers. I too drove a convertible for 12 years. Remembering the feeling of the warm sun and wind on my face. I can feel her joy!

Heather worked hard in a creative industry. As a young woman in the 70s she was employed at CBS Studios in Los Angeles where she worked as the prize inventory coordinator for The Price Is Right. It was her job to keep track of all the prizes the contestants bid on. To think about all those times I wasn't in school, due to Mom's need to have me near. It was normal to have The Price Is Right airing in the background and to think, she was as close to me as the other side of that TV screen.

**Heather**

My grandparents, Melba and Jim McKay with 15-year-old Heather

In the late 70s or early 80s, Heather was part of a class action law suit which ruled that CBS begin offering training to women employees to learn jobs that had previously been only held by men. She took a course and passed the testing to become a tape editor and then worked editing pieces that aired on the nightly news. She did this job until she retired, even winning awards for her work during the coverage of the Whittier earthquake of 1987. Heather lived in Los Angeles and then later, Malibu in a home overlooking the ocean where she enjoyed entertaining her many eclectic friends. She always seemed to have a dog. Her last one was a West Highland White Terrier named Duffy. Tragedy struck when the wildfires of 1993 burned her house down but, Heather persevered and rebuilt on the same lot creating her dream home. She lost both parents and then the love of her life shortly after — a former poetry Professor from USC she met at one of her writing workshops. She enjoyed writing poetry and prose. As I later had the opportunity to read some of her work, I suspect she found healing as pen met paper. After retirement she volunteered at a local museum as a Docent, giving guided tours and event planning for special events. She loved art that inspired her and enjoyed displaying it in her home.

I am her…and she is me. Uncanny the many parallels in our lives. After an afternoon spent gaining all this insight, I hovered in a dream state for the next several days. My recent surgery pain now much diminished as the endorphins filled my body.

# Mustang and Valentine

Back on the evening of December 7, 2019 Mustang suffered a seizure. I scooped him up and held him until it passed. The next day I rushed him to my vet, but they were stumped as they couldn't seem to diagnose what was wrong with him. They kept reassuring me that he was stable but, I knew different. Throughout December, his condition was not good. His little body was exhausted and his rapid breathing worried me terribly. He was scheduled the morning of the 23rd to go to a specialist to have an echocardiogram but, we did not make it to that appointment.

Mustang always slept right next to me, actually snuggling into the small of my back where the pressure felt reassuring. We had gone to sleep like always with little Valentine at the foot of the bed and Mustang at my side. In the middle of the night I rolled over to change positions, and when my hand touched him, I felt that he was cold. My eyes flew open and I knew immediately what had happened but I was too afraid to turn on the light to investigate. Just go back to sleep I told myself, but sleep would not come. I turned on the light and threw back the covers to see he was gone. Oh, how I cried. I even tried to massage his side to see if his little heart would start beating again. Once I was able to compose myself, I wrapped him in his Batman blanket, brought him into the living room, and placed him in his doggy bed. I didn't sleep the rest of the night. The next day I had to work and given it was two days before Christmas, I had a packed schedule. I couldn't let my customers down by canceling. Somehow, I pulled myself together enough to go downstairs and work on clients all day. I didn't tell them what I was dealing with upstairs. As my last client wished me a Merry Christmas and headed out the door, I finally allowed myself to let go. For me, losing my pets has been just as hard as losing my parents. Maybe even worse. All of that innocent unconditional love, gone so abruptly.

Now it is the summer of 2021. Little Valentine had suffered from a progressive condition called Myopathy for quite some time. It was now getting worse and her little body just couldn't do it anymore. As much as I tried, I couldn't quite bring her out of the grief over losing Mustang. Since the day I brought her home at eight weeks old, all she did was follow him around. She now lacked direction and seemed aloof not finding much joy in anything. I invested in a series of laser treatments to try to regenerate some of her nerves to improve her walk but, they didn't work and, I was carrying her constantly. Our walks were now in a doggy stroller so she could still enjoy smelling the air, watching the squirrels run up the trees and hear the birds sing. June was especially hot that year and being a pug with their breathing issues, she was not able to be outside much. But on June 21, it was cool and absolutely beautiful out. I knew that was the day. I took her for a long stroll to let her enjoy her neighborhood once more. Late that afternoon, she and I went to the Vet and I held her as she left this earth. The last thing she did before she died was look right at me as if to say, "Thank you." It was then I knew she was in pain, both emotionally and physically, and was so relieved to have it come to an end. I wasn't sure I could handle another heartbreak and, her absence drew attention to the quietness in my home that had never been. I moved into this house with three-year-old Harley and have never spent a night here without a dog or two by my side. Every noise made me jump and I'd look for excuses to leave the house as much as possible. Out of the corner of my eye, I kept thinking I saw her on the floor. Every time I'd look, I would well with sadness once again, but then immediately remember her little face thanking me. She was once again following Mustang around and I knew that's where she wanted to be.

**Valentine and Mustang**

I only lasted a few of weeks before I brought home an eight week old Bernedoodle puppy. I had researched the breed and decided with the increased crime and instability in my city, I might do better with a larger, more protective dog. Weighing in at 83 pounds full grown, he was quite a contrast from my little pugs. For a few months, he was small enough to carry around and those puppy kisses did a great job at clearing the tears. We embarked on obedience training. I knew a larger dog would give me a run for my money if I didn't get him under control from an early age. This boy was so smart! He seemed to pick up on everything the first time he was taught. One afternoon while standing at my kitchen sink washing dishes, I was talking to God, as I often do, and thanking him for always ensuring I had such amazing, wonderful dogs. How could I possibly be so fortunate to hit the jackpot time after time after time? His answer came much like the day it did while holding newborn Chase. As clear as day I heard, *"You need someone to give your heart to…"*

I love how God talks to me, always open ended making me think and wrestle with truth.

Two weeks after I brought him home, Lee Anne threw me a puppy shower. So many of my girlfriends showed up with gifts and gift cards. We ate hotdogs and cupcakes decorated with paw print icing. It was just what I needed to welcome my new pup into my life. His name is McKay after my birth-Mom's very Scottish surname. I decided to use the Scottish pronunciation "Mc-eye" just to change it up slightly. He took to his new name immediately and I would like to take that as a sign of approval from Heather.

That next Christmas a package arrived from my new found cousin Andrew with items carefully packed inside that belonged to my birth-mother. A tablecloth that she had sewn, interestingly carved chop sticks that she used when entertaining friends at her house for dinner, replicas of her awards she won for her work in tape editing, and a pair of silver jellyfish earrings that some day, maybe I'll have the courage to wear. I loved the fact that I now had some of her belongings. Things her fingers touched. In talking about these gifts with my fellow "party doll" Christy, I shared with her my insecurity about having them. I questioned whether or not Heather would want them to be in my possession. Christy's response helped me to shift my thinking. "Of course she would! That's why you have them."

Later on a trip with Lee Anne out to California, I was so fortunate to finally meet Andrew and Eric. They picked us up at our hotel and took us out for brunch to a great place with ocean views. I was so nervous… telling Lee Anne to make sure not to talk to much. This was big for me, the first time meeting family on Heather's side. They were so welcoming and gracious. We ate and enjoyed a couple of drinks, which helped the nerves, while getting to know each other a little. I left that experience wanting more of them.

# You Should Write A Book

By now, I cannot tell you how many people upon hearing about all this birth-family news have told me I should write a book. Friends, clients, neighbors, and even family. *"You SO should write a book about all of this!"* At first I would agree but honestly, did not have a clue as to how I would unpack all of this experience into writing. I have now stopped seeing my therapist. On my last visit with her she asked me the question,

*"What would it look like if you loved yourself?"*

For some reason, this question actually made me angry. I myself completely empty as to how to answer it. I know so many people who have been helped by therapy, but this type of therapy, I did not find helpful to relieve the pain that has now become such a big part of me.

In July of 2022 I went out for dinner with a couple of my girlfriends for my birthday. With glasses raised someone toasted, *"Here's to many more birthdays!"*

Surprisingly, these words made me feel sick. If this is how many more years will feel, ...please, no thank you! My response opened my eyes to the reality that I was in deep trouble. I am sinking...and I will surely drown. The very next day I started to write.

Sitting quietly with my thoughts, the stored up memories and feelings would flood from a place that I had worked so hard to shut down and silence. When I would enter into this space, my fingers would hit the keys and the outpouring of words would fill page after page. It took on an energy of its own and it's actually quite a mystery to me. I would often look back, reading what I wrote and find myself surprised. Did I write that? Yes I did...every word. Tears would literally pour to the point I would need to take long breaks to steady myself. I felt such anger as my adult self relived my childhood memories, wishing I had been there to protect that sad little girl with the freckles. My harsh *"FUCK YOU!!"* screamed at unsuspecting neighborhood girls, when it was honestly intended for my parents. Writing has produced way more processing than anything else I've ever tried. And, in my writing I was able to see things from an outside perspective that allowed insight to further forgive my parents. Realizing that they too were broken.

In early 2023 after much discussion, I booked a flight to go visit Heather's relatives who all lived in Vancouver, Canada. This is where my great grandparents immigrated from Scotland and where Heather was born and spent her first 15 years. Now, I will meet Cheryl face-to-face. The one who made this discovery all possible. She along with her sister Deborah, both of them my first cousins once removed, their kids and even a couple of third cousins. Cheryl's stepmother Helen was the wife of my great uncle, to which she and he had a very close relationship with Heather. My great uncle George, a retired documentary writer with the CBC created and delivered her beautiful eulogy.

With George's recent passing, Helen was now living by herself in their large home. She invited me to come stay with her over Mother's Day weekend. There we would celebrate her husband, gone after a lengthy battle with Alzheimer's, and the discovery of me.

The whole family would be invited over and I would get a chance to meet them all. By now, I have been writing for months and my heart is feeling much lighter. I embrace this opportunity and quickly secure airfare. I flew out the Thursday before Mother's Day, and actually felt no fear. I was so excited to meet the ones important and loved by my birth-Mom. Texting with Helen the days leading up to my arrival, I had offered to come out to her car when I got there to make things easier, to which she replied… *"Oh, no! I will come in and collect you. I'll be wearing a tan hat with a black band."* As I deplane, making my way through customs and security, I come out to the large area where guests can pick up travelers. As I walked, I scanned the crowd searching for the tan hat with the black band. And then I see her! Waving at her with my biggest smile, I see her wiping her eyes. We walked side-by-side with a half wall separating us for quite some time before we could come together and embrace. She is now fully crying and hugging me tightly… *"Oh, my! You look even more like her in person."* I could see in her eyes, her statement was true. Up until now, I had held it together…but I am now sobbing as well. I took her hands in mine, and thanked her for helping make a dream come true. We drove from the airport to the west side of town where Helen lives. Wow! Vancouver is stunning…my birth-Mom's birthplace and hometown. Once we arrive, she shows me the comfortable guest room I will be staying in. The room my mother stayed in as well when she came to visit! Everything about this house was so beautiful and perfect. It carried a balance between elegance and warmth. As I set my luggage down on the bed, a beautiful vase of fresh cut tulips sits on the dresser welcoming me. These are my people! I can feel it.

As I sit with my new found cousin Cheryl and with Helen, they shared with me memories and insights about Heather. As these things were spoken, I'd metaphorically grab them out of the air and press them deep in to my heart. So many of her traits I share. My inner dialogue was constantly saying, That's why… fill in the blank. Helen gave me a copy of Heather's eulogy that her husband had written. It describes how sweet of a child she was and what a strong, determined woman she became — carving out an exciting career in a male dominated industry, where she excelled and shined! I feel so proud to be from her. While driving in the car, Helen tells me…

*"She could have been successful in many fields. Everything she did was done with determination and excellence. Whatever she touched, she did it fully."*

Heather

Once home, I was sharing this exchange with Lee Anne. She chuckled and said, *"Barb, that is exactly how I would describe you!"* And then she launched into many descriptions of this example witnessed in our decades long friendship. Another gem to proudly wear.

My second day there, the caterers came, the dishes were set out, and the guests started to arrive. Both Cheryl and Deborah's ex-husband's wanted to come. They both had many memories of Heather... flying down to LA on vacation to take their kids to Disneyland and staying at her place. I heard fun stories of dinner parties where the wine and conversation would flow. They too were curious about this secret child Heather never shared about. As Cheryl's ex husband walked in I recognized the shock on his face as he sees me. Later when we talked, he told me the resemblance was uncanny, even down to our mannerisms. Each time I hear such remarks, it's like another crack in my heart gets healed.

On my last day in Canada, Deborah was there with her two sons, playing her guitar and encouraging us to sing and harmonize along with her. We fumbled around a little with some Joni Mitchell songs.

Deborah is so talented. I'm afraid my jumping in didn't do them much justice, yet, it was such a bright moment.

Many of the family and other guests that I had the opportunity to meet while I was there told me, *"You're so brave to do this!"* I did not recognize this as bravery. It came from a place beyond myself that literally pushed me out of the way to go after. A part of me needed to prove to myself that I came from something good, something beautiful. I honestly had no choice but to go along for the ride.

While discovering who my birth-Dad was, what largely stood out to me was how proud I felt. Pride in my rich Mexican heritage. Pride in the fact that I come from such down to earth, hard-working people. Their work ethic, thankfully shared with me. Pride that my ancestors came from such extreme persecution and torture to rebuild their lives and rise above. That strength, I have felt it all along. This type of expression of pride was so new and beautiful to me. My ability to easily assemble furniture comes from my crafty Machinist Dad. My love of gardening, passed down from my determined grandmother Ester. My freckles, my eyes…

And now calling myself a Medina, nothing can ever take that away from me.

Now, just coming home from meeting my Mom's family, what I take away from this experience is a newfound acceptance. In hearing about her life, her accomplishments and triumphs, her heart breaks… I see such an incredibly strong, out of the ordinary, amazing person. And if she was out of the ordinary and amazing, I must be too — because I'm her daughter.

In all honesty, I have to admit that I have struggled to feel I deserve to be on this earth my entire life. The first impression I remember recognizing from both of my parents was the need for me to stay quiet, don't get in the way, pretend I'm not there, do as I'm told. I realize how I have abandon myself. Retreating into a small place not to share myself with others. But now, I can start to apply some of this goodness and light of where I come from to myself. I feel the beginnings of a nudge to step forward. To wear this discovery proudly. To forgive myself, and start allowing permission to get acquainted with who I am and acknowledge all the beauty that is there. Beauty that others have always seen but, I have been blinded too.

All these years later, I still maintain those early friendships and relationships. I continue to add to them with many more amazing people that I carefully bring into my life — my appointed family. My friend's kids I've watched grow up into bright individuals. And my close bond with Chase continues even now as he approaches 30. I'm so proud of the thoughtful, integrity filled, beautiful man he has become. And, I'd like to think I had a little something to do with that...

Helen introduced me to some photos of my Mom I had not seen before and one in particular took my breath away. It was a candid shot of her snuggling with her dog. A moment caught without pose. As her pup licks her cheek, she leans slightly into it with a content look that I recognize all so well. I get you Heather. I know this moment because I too have experienced it so many times. An immediate connection.

Heather

The piece of my heart that was always meant for her is finally able to awaken, and I can feel it beating.

My lifelong self-loathing does not fit in with this new outlook anymore so, maybe I can begin to imagine myself letting that go. I no longer need to apologize for who I am, or to shrink down my existence like I had growing up in order to survive. Perhaps, with this new lens, I can start to see myself in a different light. Maybe, instead of self-loath, I can begin to make friends with who I was meant to be all along.

Besides music, nothing has brought such relief to my heart and nervous system more than writing. I realize why I faithfully journaled from the ages of 13 to 22. Writing saved my life...and it seems to still have that ability. As I write and these thoughts transfer onto the page, my heart's heaviness is lifted. The more I write, the lighter it feels. Once I leave it on the page, I can turn and walk away from it, knowing it is safe and kept. I also recognize why my desperate prayers for rescue were not answered. Sitting in such pain these recent years was allowed so that this precious, vulnerable, and delicate story would not be forgotten. My pain was the cost of protecting it. And now, as my fingers leave the keyboard, I can dream of the possibility that I will no longer need to tread deep water, and that maybe, it's time to swim.

THE END

*I was patient while I waited for the Lord.*
*He turned to me and heard my cry for help.*
*I was sliding down into the pit of death, and*
*He pulled me out.*
*He brought me up out of the mud and dirt.*
*He set my feet on a rock.*
*He gave me a firm place to stand on.*

Psalm 40:1-2

# About the Author

Barbara Medina originally hails from Southern California, spending her first 12 years there. She later landed in the Twin Cities of Minnesota where she continues to live today. After finishing high school, she eventually attended Cosmetology school and has worked as a Hairstylist for 37 years within the industry… Behind the chair, in management and also as an educator. After discovering birth-family information, she was led on a journey that forced her to write about her experiences as she processed along the way. Calling it all, "not for the faint of heart." Writing for publication is a first for her. After sharing her "first draft" with selected individuals within her inner circle, the feedback was so overwhelmingly positive that she continued working on her novel until she was satisfied with her expression of the events written about. She shares her story with the hope of helping others who might share in relating to being a child of adoption and the desire for self discovery. Barbara currently lives in Minneapolis with her three year old Bernedoodle McKay, where she still enjoys her career doing hair and making her clients happy.

Made in the USA
Monee, IL
11 December 2024